THE COMPLETE
Kabbalah
COURSE

THE COMPLETE

Kabbalah

COURSE

Practical exercises to reach
your inner and upper worlds

PAUL ROLAND

Foreword by Z'ev ben Shimon Halevi

quantum

LONDON • NEW YORK • TORONTO • SYDNEY

quantum

An imprint of W. Foulsham & Co. Ltd
The Publishing House, Bennetts Close, Cippenham, Slough,
Berkshire, SL1 5AP, England

ISBN 0-572-03127-0

Cover photograph by Jurgen Ziewe

Photographs of the artwork by Sylvia Gainsford from *The Kabbalah Cards* reproduced by permission of AGM AGMüller Urania, Bahnhofstrasse 21, CH8212 Neuhasen am Reinfall, Switzerland

A CIP record for this book is available from the British Library

Disclaimer
The exercises in this book are intended for relaxation and increasing self-awareness. However, if you have recently experienced mental or emotional problems or are taking strong medication you should seek professional medical advice before practising these meditations and visualisations on your own. The author and publisher accept no responsibility for any harm caused by or to anyone as a result of the misuse of these exercises. These exercises should never be attempted while under the influence of alcohol or drugs of any kind. Nor should they be practised by anyone in a psychologically disturbed state of mind.

Printed in Great Britain by Creative Print and Design (Wales), Ebbw Vale

Contents

Dedication

The author respectfully dedicates this book to Z'ev ben Shimon Halevi and gratefully acknowledges the insights gleaned from *The Work of the Kabbalist*, which has proven an inspiration for the current work.

Author's note

In accordance with tradition, I am obliged to state that what follows is my personal interpretation of the teachings, obtained through study, personal experience and insight. My views do not necessarily correspond with those of other initiates.

There are several spellings of the word Kabbalah. It is generally accepted that Kabbalah denotes the traditional teachings, while Cabbala refers to the Christian revisionist version, and Qabalah to the occult or magical offshoot.

According to tradition, dates are denoted as being either BCE (Before Common Era aka BC) or CE (Common Era aka AD), as Judaism does not acknowledge the terms 'Before Christ' and 'Anno Domini'.

About the author

Paul Roland is a teacher of spiritual development and Kabbalistic meditation. He is also the creator of the Kabbalah Cards (AGM AGMüller Urania) and the author of more than a dozen books, including *How Psychic Are You?* (Hamlyn), *Meditation Solutions* (Hamlyn), *Investigating the Unexplained* (Piatkus) and *Contact Your Guardian Angel* (Quantum/Foulsham). His work has been translated into several languages, including Hebrew, Hungarian, German, French, Norwegian, Dutch, Russian, Spanish and Portuguese.

His own mystic experiences began when he was still a child and led him to study various aspects of the esoteric, including yoga, meditation, Buddhism and the Kabbalah, the latter with one of the foremost Masters of our time.

For more information visit www.paulroland.co.uk.

Foreword

This Paul Roland book is an impressive work. It has scholarship, theory and practice as well as strong feelings of love for this ancient and complex esoteric system. There are many publications now on Kabbalah, but most do not penetrate its seemingly obscure surface beyond what the author has read or heard. In this volume, there has been a thorough investigation into the subject from many angles, ranging from the traditional Jewish Orthodox view to the Western Occult approach. However, the main theme of human evolution, the cosmos and their relationship to the divine is never forgotten. That is the mark of a Kabbalist as against a learned scholar or well-researched writer.

This is indicated by the excellent exercises, which are clearly based upon personal experience. Moreover, the many anecdotes that illustrate Kabbalistic principles illuminate the metaphysics and symbolism of seemingly obscure archetypes. This brings them into the ken of consciousness as well as relating them to everyday life. The cross-referencing to various traditions is most important so as to see connections and a different way of perceiving the same factor. Of equal importance is the prudent implication not to discard common sense. This is vital, as many texts on Kabbalah and allied occult subjects show how to open the door to the invisible world, but not how to contain what might come in. The Jewish sages said that one should be mature before taking up Kabbalah. Just as important, a Kabbalist should be well versed in learning and balanced in practice. This book has these elements and can be used to gain insight and wisdom, not power, which is the chief temptation of anyone who might wish to become an initiate for the wrong reason. I recommend this book, which should be used with careful consideration, as Kabbalah has been known to change the course of a life.

Z'ev ben Shimon Halevi

Introduction

Kabbalah is the ancient Jewish mystical system whose teachings lie at the heart of the Western esoteric tradition. It seeks to answer the key questions that preoccupy us all concerning the meaning of life and the nature of existence, while at the same time offering profound insights into the human psyche and providing techniques for personal transformation.

Its central premise states that we are all, in essence, divine, and that we have the free will to rise to the level of the angels or descend to the level of the beasts. Kabbalah celebrates individuality and discourages blind faith and any form of belief system that encourages its followers to delegate responsibility for their spiritual development to someone else. It condemns the personality cults that often surround gurus and charismatic religious leaders and discourages any practice that could be considered superficial or elitist, such as the wearing of red strings around the wrist, which has recently become fashionable among celebrity converts. In fact, the wearing of a red string around the wrist is expressly forbidden by the Tosefta (an early Talmudic text). In Shabbat 7–8 it is stated that such practices are 'darchei emori' meaning 'a worthless superstition'.

It is for each of us to determine our own destiny, to attain self-realisation and thereby contribute to the well-being of the world and the evolution of the human species. Alternatively, we can indulge our baser instincts and submit to our fears, which is a denial of our divine potential and the very definition of evil – for Kabbalah contends that there is no conscious malevolent entity at work in the universe contravening the divine will, only ourselves. Our present problems are therefore seen as symptomatic of an evolutionary struggle between those in search of their divine nature and those in denial of it, rather than as a manifestation of an apocalyptic battle between cosmic forces. Evil is defined in purely evolutionary terms as that which disintegrates and disperses energy and matter back into their primary elements, for nothing can be actually destroyed, only changed. Evil is therefore a contrary impulse to evolution, a checking, constraining factor, testing our integrity and willpower. To those whose lives are disrupted by an evil act, the psychological and emotional impact can be considerable, but all injustices are ultimately addressed by the universal law of cause and effect (karma), whether it be in this lifetime or the next.

In this present age of religious extremism and increasing intolerance, Kabbalah advances a positive philosophy in which every individual is significant and empowered with the means of attaining liberation from the cycle of birth and death. To do this we can draw upon the inner guidance of our Higher Self or Holy Guardian Angel using techniques that are detailed in the following pages. Incidentally, no knowledge of Judaism is needed in order to practise these techniques nor to benefit from this ageless wisdom. In fact, it is the duty of every generation to reinterpret the Kabbalah's teachings for their own time and in their own terms, as long as they remain faithful to its principles.

Kabbalah does not demand blind faith, nor does it require initiates to retire to a remote spiritual retreat and renounce the pleasures of the material world. In fact, it actively encourages practitioners to immerse themselves in life-affirming activities, for only in the give and take of human relationships can we hope to grow and learn about ourselves through our interaction with others. Anyone who seeks escape from responsibility or from reality should look elsewhere. Kabbalah does not offer a quick spiritual fix. Neither is it an impenetrable metaphysical system based on arcane biblical theories. It is rather a divinely simple and practical means to spiritual growth and self-awareness. It seeks to explain what lies behind the apparent chaos, injustice and random cruelty of our world, and in doing so reveals the purpose of life and the path that leads to our divine destiny. For that reason it is imperative that its secrets should now be revealed for the enlightenment of all those who wish to connect with their true nature, for the truth is that we can only change the world if we first change ourselves.

It is important to state at the outset that Kabbalah is not the only way and its practitioners do not claim exclusive rights to the truth, but it is unique in the way it conceptualises the mysteries of existence and then offers the means by which anyone can test the validity of the teachings for themselves. In the following pages you will find dozens of original visualisations and practical exercises so that you can experience the inner and upper worlds through heightened states of consciousness and explore the symbolic landscape of your own psyche to awaken the divine within.

Such secrets were initially encoded in the myths of the Old Testament and in religious ritual that formed the exoteric (outer) practices of orthodox Judaism, while their esoteric (hidden) significance was lost with the passing of the centuries.

This universal truth, that we are all responsible for our own 'salvation', is at the heart of occult philosophy and is encoded in the teachings of the masters. It is thought that the dissemination of this knowledge was the true mission of Joshua ben Miriam, more commonly known as Jesus of Nazareth, who expressed the concept in the phrase 'the Kingdom of heaven is within you'.

All of the major religions initially inspired the faithful to seek for truth and meaning in life, but over time they became preoccupied less with the spirit than with the letter of the law that bound the community to formal, collective worship. Without orthodox religion, civilisation would have descended into chaos centuries ago. Its moral precepts helped to form the foundation of Western society and endorsed our ancestors' belief in righteous living. Unfortunately, in many cases righteousness begat self-righteousness and the zeal to save others from themselves whether they wanted to be saved or not. Many extremists set themselves up as mediators between man and God, and in their zeal some assumed the role of divine authority, to become the antithesis of what the founders of their religion had taught. Today orthodox religion can still offer believers comfort and guidance in difficult times, but an increasing number of people feel the need to seek out the truth for themselves and they prefer to travel with their eyes open rather than be led to the promised land. For them Kabbalah offers a means for attaining that direct, personal experience of the divine.

By the Middle Ages Kabbalah had become synonymous in the fervid public imagination with ceremonial magic, which provided an excuse for a succession of pogroms against the Jews. It is thought that in an effort to conceal their secrets initiates may have encoded their teachings in the Tarot cards (of which more in Chapter 10).

In the 19th century, thanks to the profane practices of such charlatans as the notorious magician Aleister Crowley and the empty theatricals of his contemporaries in the Golden Dawn, the stigma of occultism had firmly adhered to anything relating to the Kabbalah, and consequently the teachings fell into disrepute.

Until the latter years of the 20th century, Kabbalah was considered suspect or, at worst, superstitious nonsense by orthodox Jews, and as arcane, wilfully obscure and impenetrable by all but the most dedicated mystic. Now it is enjoying a revival and the attendant publicity that inevitably comes with the acquisition of celebrity converts such as pop priestess Madonna and a host of Hollywood film stars.

In a world of increasing insecurity and disillusionment with traditional religions, it was perhaps inevitable that the Kabbalah would be seized upon as the next New Age fad. Part of our current malady stems from the realisation that we cannot believe in a patriarchal creator who will reach down out of the sky to punish the sinners and reward the faithful. We are more sophisticated than that, and yet we still hope that there is a greater reality than the one into which we have been born.

In contrast to the often abstract philosophies of the East, Kabbalah offers a pragmatic alternative, one in which the divine is manifest in the world around us and in each and every human being in finite form. If we wish to understand the will and nature of the creator we have only to look within, and if we desire truly to know ourselves we only have to look at the world we have created. In Kabbalah our spiritual and psychological needs are finally reconciled.

Note on the exercises

All exercises can be performed either seated or lying down unless otherwise stated. It is recommended that you record the instructions for the longer visualisations, or ask a friend to read them aloud, so that you do not have to refer to them during the exercise. In time, as you become familiar with the structure of the exercises, you will be able to perform them without any assistance.

1

A Brief History of Kabbalah

The origins of Kabbalah, also known as The Work of Unification, are obscure, though it appears to have developed between the 6th century BCE and the 1st century CE from an earlier tradition known as Maaseh Merkabah (The Work of The Chariot), the chariot being symbolic of the mental platform created by intense meditation and prayer on which the initiate would ascend through the halls of heaven to commune with the divine. Attaining altered states of consciousness for the purposes of enlightenment was considered a sacred act for which much painstaking preparation had to be made to ensure that the traveller was not unbalanced by what they glimpsed of the upper worlds and their inhabitants. Today such precautions are still considered prudent, as even a momentary glimpse of the greater reality can disturb those who are not psychologically sound and securely grounded.

Techniques for attaining altered states of consciousness are alluded to in both the Babylonian and the Palestinian Talmud, books of Jewish religious instruction that date from the 1st century CE. However, such practices are thought to have originated thousands of years earlier, as the Talmud of the 1st century CE is compiled from much earlier texts of an indeterminate age. Biblical commentaries suggest that both the male and female founders of the Jewish faith communed with the divine using various techniques, including mantras, prayer, intense study of the Hebrew letters and invocation of the divine presence using a combination of holy names, a process known as Maaseh Bereshet (The Work of Creation).

The Essenes (200 BCE–200 CE)

In biblical times Merkabah would have been practised mainly by the initiates of the numerous ascetic sects, who established isolated communities throughout Palestine. The most significant of these were the Essenes, who founded one of the first Kabbalistic monasteries at Qumran, in what is now Jordan, and the Nazarenes, of whom Joshua ben Miriam, more commonly known as Jesus, is believed to have been an initiate.

Such sects are known to have placed great emphasis on the mastering of physical postures similar to the asanas of yoga and on exercises designed to stimulate the etheric energy centres of the human body, which are now commonly referred to by their Sanskrit name of chakras.

As a focus for their meditations, the members of these ascetic sects devised a symbol which they called the Tree of Life, comprising seven branches stretching skywards and seven roots penetrating the earth, with man representing the trunk, the purpose of contemplation being the syntheses of the celestial and terrestrial forces within the body.

These they named the seven angels of the physical world (the angels of the Sun, Fire, Water, Air, Earth, Joy and the Earthly Mother) and the seven angels of Heaven (the angels of Power, Life, Love, Wisdom, Work, Peace and the Heavenly Father), which are compatible with the divine Attributes of the Kabbalistic system.

Sacred texts

The early Jewish mystics of Babylon, Hellenistic Egypt and Roman-occupied Judea, including the Essenes and the Nazarenes, believed that they had been entrusted with the secrets of existence by God, whose archangel, Raziel, had imparted them to Adam in the Garden of Eden in order that human kind could find its way back to Paradise. So fearful were they that such secrets might become known to the uninitiated that they refused to write anything down. Instead they determined that the teachings must became an exclusively oral tradition, imparted personally from teacher to pupil, a practice which gives the teachings their name, for Kabbalah means 'to receive'.

The first of the three cornerstones of Kabbalistic literature appeared in the 3rd-century CE. The *Sefer ha Yetzirah (The Book of Creation)* is an anonymous work attributed to Rabbi Akiba. It describes a universe inhabited by angels and demons largely derived from Babylonian cosmology and provides meditations on the mystical significance of the Hebrew alphabet. A central theme of the *Sefer ha Yetzirah* is that words have an innate power and that to know the secret name of God is to possess the means of creation, a concept that was later echoed in the Christian concept of 'the word'.

The power of the word was central to Kabbalistic meditation during the Middle Ages, particularly the secret names of God, each one of which denoted a different aspect of his being. One of the most influential figures of this period was Abraham Abulafia (1240–95), who used permutations of Hebrew letters in meditation to attain ecstatic states, in a similar way that Buddhists use mantras.

The *Sefer ha Yetzirah* can be considered one of the three pillars of Kabbalistic literature, the others being the *Sefer ha Zohar (The Book of Splendour)* and the *Sefer Torah (The Book of the Law)*, which is more commonly known as the Old Testament. The *Zohar* was compiled from 1,000 years of oral teachings by Rabbi Moses ben Shemtov of Leon and circulated at the end of the 13th century in Spain, where it inspired a golden age of rabbinical scholarship. Its commentaries on the hidden meanings of the *Torah* are interpreted as stating that every individual is a personification of the divine spark, a living aspect of God, who manifests through us in order to determine the course of his creation.

This theme was taken up by the 16th-century Kabbalist Moses Cordovero, whose influential works *The Garden of Pomegranates* and *The Palm Tree of Deborah* describe how we can assist the divine through our actions and the practice of righteous living.

It was Isaac Luria, a pupil of Cordovero, who was responsible for splitting the tradition along two distinctly separate and incompatible lines, which continue to this day. He theorised that evil is a conscious entity that emerged from the shattered vessels of an early attempt to create the universe and now exists as a shadow of our own universe, known as the Kellipot (Kingdom of Shells). This idea, which became known as the Lurianic tradition, found favour with ultra-orthodox Hasidic Jews and with those who practised ritual magic. In contrast, the older branch of Kabbalah, known as the Toledano tradition (because it flourished near Toledo in Spain during the Middle Ages), is founded on the belief that God and all that he created is perfect and that evil is the wilful abuse of our free will. The Toledano tradition continues to thrive in parallel with the more fatalistic Lurianic tradition.

The sefirotic scheme that we are familiar with today is believed to have been created by Isaac the Blind (c.1160–1236 CE) in order to answer the key questions, 'If God made the world, then what is the world if not God?' and 'If the world is God, why is it not perfect?' According to the 20th-century writer Gershom Scholem, Isaac also devised the concept of the lightning flash, in which the divine light is said to have been diluted in stages – a theory that has much in common with the Neoplatonic concept of a 'chain of being', with our physical universe as the last link in the chain. Scholem also credits Isaac the Blind with coining the term Kabbalah to distinguish the teachings from the earlier Merkabah.

Christian Cabbalists

By the Middle Ages the Hokhmah Nistarah (Hidden Wisdom) had travelled to Europe, where it developed along two distinct lines: one in which its practical applications were adopted as the foundation for ritual magic and the other in which its theoretical aspects were explored in order to speculate on the nature of God.

Three hundred years later, during the Renaissance, there arose several brilliant philosophers who sought to combine the two lines of development in the hope of decoding the mysteries of life, among them Agrippa Von Nettesheim and Paracelsus. Both viewed science and the occult as two aspects of the same discipline and in doing so laid the foundations for modern chemistry, physics and medicine.

Unfortunately, and perhaps predictably, many of their contemporaries were not so independently minded. Christian scholars Giovanni Pico della Mirandola and Johann Reuchlin were so anxious to appease the Church authorities that they enlisted the assistance of converted Jews to decode the secrets of the sefirotic Tree in an attempt to prove that Kabbalah contained proof of Christ's divinity.

Mirandola's zeal was not appreciated by his patrons, and in 1486 he was condemned as a heretic for declaring that 'Angels only understand Hebrew' and asserting that 'Magic is the highest and holiest form of philosophy'.

Reuchlin fared little better after publishing *The Bible of the Christian Cabala*, in which he stated that God had 'revealed His secrets to Man in Hebrew' and that Kabbalah was 'a symbolic theology, in which letters and names are not only the signs for things, but also their very essence'. After years studying original Hebrew manuscripts donated by grateful rabbis whom he had saved from persecution, he concluded that Kabbalah was a sublime expression of the universal truth at the heart of all religions. It was a sentiment that did not find favour with the papal authorities.

In their eagerness to prove that Christianity was the natural successor to Judaism, the Christian Cabbalists of the 15th century wilfully misinterpreted the teachings for their own ends. However, it is patently obvious that the Christian concept of original sin is incompatible with the Kabbalistic principle, which states that we are only separated from the source through the denial of our divine nature.

Moreover, the central credo of Christianity is that no-one can enter the kingdom of heaven until they accept Jesus as the Son of God and their saviour, which is in contrast to the belief held by followers of Kabbalah, who view Jesus as one of many enlightened teachers who have appeared through the ages to act as living proof that every human being is responsible for and capable of attaining their own salvation.

Freemasonry (17th century)

Anyone familiar with the symbols and rituals of Freemasonry will recognise key elements from the Kabbalah, most notably the presence of the two pillars at the entrance to every Masonic temple and again in the Main Hall. The chequered floor of the central chamber represents the duality of divine forces: energy and matter, active and passive, male and female – a concept central to Kabbalah – while the main teaching aid, known as the Tracing Board, depicts God as the Great Architect of the Universe, his name inscribed in Hebrew. The Kabbalistic concept of the physical universe being a reflection of the upper worlds is represented by a symbolic diagram showing the temple guarded by the sun and the moon. Underneath is Jacob's ladder, symbol of our ability to ascend to a higher plane, the three rungs representing faith, hope and charity, the attributes required of the members at each level of initiation.

It is assumed that the founders of Freemasonary adopted Kabbalistic concepts in the belief that they were custodians of secrets dating back to the time of Solomon's Temple. In doing so, they integrated sound principles for righteous living into the rites of a philanthropic secret society and preserved its teachings, albeit in their own terminology.

In the ritual of the Second Degree, for example, the initiate is told that every building we design and construct mirrors the divine process of creation. The 'regular progression of science from a point to a line, from a line to a plane, from a plane to a solid' reveals that everything we create embodies the essence of that which preceded it in the same way that our world is the physical manifestation of the higher worlds, which served as its blueprint.

The Hermetic Order of the Golden Dawn (19th century)

Although the founders of the Golden Dawn may have considered themselves modern-day mystics in search of enlightenment, the majority of the members of this Victorian secret society were seduced by the promise of being witness to psychic phenomena and bullied into obedience by overbearing personalities such as the notorious magician Aleisteir Crowley and the eccentric occultist MacGregor Mathers (author of *The Kabbalah Unveiled*).

The most eminent members, including the poet W.B. Yeats and several leading lights of the scientific establishment, were no doubt sincere in their search for insights and new experiences, but the majority viewed the confusion of Kabbalistic symbols, Egyptian magic, Enochian angel invocations and Rosicrucian rituals as little more than exotic window dressing for their highly theatrical ceremonies.

It is partly due to the melodramatic antics of the Golden Dawn and pompous self-appointed 'experts' of the period, such as Eliphas Levi and A.E. Waite, that Kabbalah acquired a dubious reputation, which persisted well into the next century.

Much of what is taught today in esoteric groups outside the Jewish tradition is strongly influenced by the Golden Dawn and also by the writings of one of its less credulous members, leading English occultist Dion Fortune (1890–1946), author of *The Mystical Qabalah*. If you intend to read her books, you need to appreciate that her understanding was coloured by Theosophy, which was a mish-mash of Egyptian magic and Eastern philosophy tainted by fanciful notions, such as the superiority of the Aryan race and the existence of cosmic rays and the lost city of Atlantis.

Modern Kabbalah

Kabbalah's claim to be a living tradition adaptable to the needs of each generation is borne out by its revival in the 21st century. Modern masters such as Z'ev ben Shimon Halevi have reinterpreted the teachings in the light of Jungian psychology to present them as a means of personal development, whilst remaining true to the tradition. By reconciling the spiritual and psychological aspects they encourage their students to explore their inner world as a microcosm of the greater reality.

Although it is regrettable that the attentions of celebrity converts has focused media attention on the more eccentric aspects of Kabbalah (which, incidentally, are the invention of specific sects and have nothing to do with traditional Kabbalah), it is necessary to make the teachings accessible to all those who can contribute to the work. At this moment in our history it is vital to awaken as many people as possible to their true nature so as to counterbalance the upsurge of violence and religious fundamentalism that threatens to drag us into a new dark age.

2

'As Above, So Below'

According to Kabbalistic cosmology, the universe came into existence because God, the transcendent, wished to know himself, to express his love through the act of creation and to experience what he had created by manifesting in the worlds he had made. To do so he withdrew, leaving a void in which was generated the universal life force in the form of a lightning bolt. This divine light was refracted as through a prism at ten different levels of increasing density before earthing itself in matter (see diagram below).

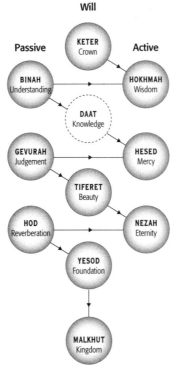

Path of the lightning bolt

What was once pure consciousness had condensed, and the divine unity was now manifest in a multiplicity of forms. Every atom, every element and every life form in the universe is therefore an expression of the divine. At various stages in the development of Kabbalah, the ten divine aspects have been expressed as lights, colours and sounds (the latter reinforcing the significance of harmony in the universe and in ourselves). But they are more traditionally symbolised as spheres known as *sefirot* (singular form *sefirah*), which, significantly, correspond with human attributes, for we are the highest expression of the divine in finite form.

Many traditions and belief systems have shared the Kabbalistic concept of creation in principle, but Kabbalah is unique in that it envisages the descent of the divine in terms of interpenetrating and interdependent stages of consciousness in descending order of emanation. As such, the Tree of Life, the central symbol of Kabbalah, on which the sefirot are arranged, can be seen as illustrating the DNA-like structure or pattern of all that emanated from the godhead, as expressed in both the macrocosm (the universe) and the microcosm (man).

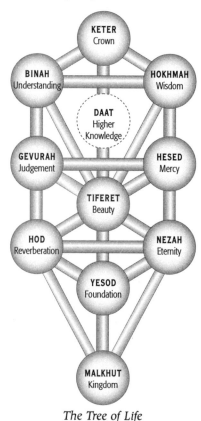

The Tree of Life

Each sefirah symbolises the active male and passive female attributes of the creator and all that it created, abstract characteristics that are beyond human comprehension. However, for practical purposes we can consider the sefirot as personifying the characteristics of a transcendent supreme being, Adam Kadmon, the Cosmic Man of Jewish mythology, of whom each human is said to be a cell. (This primordial Adam is not to be confused with the Adam in the Biblical Garden of Eden).

As a reflection of Adam Kadmon we, too, can be said to possess all the divine qualities: the Divine Connection (Keter), Wisdom (Hokhmah), Understanding (Binah), Mercy (Hesed), Justice (Gevurah), Compassion (Tiferet), Sensuality (Nezah), Intelligence (Hod), Self-Awareness (Yesod) and a physical form (Malkuth).

You will note that these attributes differ slightly from those indicated on the diagram of the Tree. This is because the traditional Hebrew names do not have a direct equivalent in modern English.

Although ten spheres are visualised on the Tree, another, Daat (Higher Knowledge), is shown on the middle pillar between Keter and Tiferet as a broken circle to indicate that it is the unmanifest gateway to the realm of the divine. It can be seen as the window between the worlds or as the abyss, to borrow a magical term, that we must cross to become an adept.

The sefirot are arranged upon three pillars (the Pillar of Equilibrium, the Pillar of Severity and the Pillar of Mercy), which symbolise the unmanifest divine principles that govern them.

It should be noted that in this context 'male' and 'female' have nothing to do with gender, nor are they mutually exclusive. We all have both male and female characteristics. In the context of the Tree, this polarity merely denotes the duality of the governing principles at work in the universe.

The principle of balance

The key theme in Kabbalah is balance, as the attributes that were held in perfect alignment in the higher realms are subject to distortion and imbalance on Earth. We may possess the same complementary qualities as the creator, but we are constantly at the mercy of our mutable emotions, our distorted sense of reality and the conflict between spiritual aspiration and physical indulgence, because while we are incarnate we are, literally, unconscious of our divine nature.

When the divine attributes symbolised by the sefirot are out of balance in the individual this can express itself in the physical symptoms of dis-ease or in psychological problems. For example, in the individual an imbalance of the sefirot Justice and Mercy at the mental level could lead either to indecision, if the imbalance was in favour of Mercy, or to stifling self-criticism if the swing was towards Judgement.

Taken down to a more mundane level an imbalance of the same sefirot could result in either fastidiousness or slovenliness, whereas the quality we should be aiming for between being overly critical on the one hand and too casual on the other is self-discipline.

At a social level, a community or state (functioning as a group soul) that emphasises Judgement without due regard for Mercy will develop a draconian judicial system in which petty offences will be punished by disproportionately severe sentences. But if the state is inclined too much towards Mercy this will lead to an extremely lenient and indulgent judicial system that is so obsessed with being seen to be fair to offenders that it loses sight of its obligations and responsibilities to protect their victims.

The aim of the Kabbalist is to balance these complementary qualities and in doing so attain self-realisation: to become the perfected human being who manifests their divine nature and perceives the divine in all things. When we have all attained this level of enlightenment, God will behold God and the cosmic cycle will be complete. At this moment of supreme self-realisation every being will understand the true meaning of the secret name of the creator, EHYEH ASHER EHYEH (I AM THAT I AM), a name that holds a multiplicity of meaning for those who contemplate its significance.

The creation of the universe can be compared to our own creative process. We begin with an idea and the will to bring it into being. We then

24

define the form by visualising it in our mind or by drawing up plans. Then we choose the materials and consider the processes involved before making whatever we had in mind into a reality.

Everything in nature and everything that we create – from our own children to the machines we invent – follows the same process and is a manifestation of our divine ability to conceive an idea, call it forth by our will, form it and make it.

In practice, every idea follows the sefirotic scheme from conception at Keter to manifestation at Malkhut. Keter is the origin of ideas. Hokhmah takes the seed of the idea and considers the other options. At Binah we question the validity of what we are proposing and ask ourselves if we understand and appreciate what is involved and what will be demanded of us. If it is both practical and sufficiently appealing, the idea then passes from the realm of ideas down through Daat to the emotional triad, where we empower it with our enthusiasm, determination and drive at Hesed and check ourselves at Gevurah to make sure. Next we put the idea to our True Self at Tiferet to ensure it is the right thing to do. Having obtained 'parental approval' from Tiferet, we then plan the practical steps at Nezah, and rationalise and justify our actions at Hod. Finally, at Yesod we consider how the idea might advance our ambitions, how our friends and family will view us if we see it through, and what it will mean if we fail. If it serves our interest or we persuade our ego to serve the greater will, the order will go forth to Malkhut, 'Take action.'

During this inner dialogue, which can take anything from a few seconds to several weeks, we may alter the original idea drastically to accommodate and appease our internal committee, or we may pass it unopposed.

Exercise: Tree of ideas

Recall an occasion when you had to debate the pros and cons of an idea before making a decision. Then use the example above to trace its path from sphere to sphere.

The nature of God

'I am God, you are God. The only difference is that I know it and you do not.' Although this statement is attributed to an Indian mystic, Sri Satya Sai Baba, it sums up a controversial concept expounded by some modern Kabbalists. For these individuals, God is not an ancient, bearded patriarchal figure who sits on a celestial throne judging humankind, rewarding good deeds and punishing the wicked. God is consciousness, the

25

divine spark within every human being, although the source of this force may exist as a separate entity (AYIN, literally 'No Thing') beyond existence in the divine dimension of pure spirit.

Such a concept would have been considered blasphemous 100 years ago – and may still be considered so by orthodox and even liberal Jews, who view God as a transcendent presence to be feared and loved. Even today it is forbidden for Jews to depict the image of God in any form other than as a light or an amorphous presence in art or in objects of worship. But contemporary Kabbalah has discarded the trappings of superstition and a long association with magic, which had led orthodox Jews to condemn it as heretical. The modern Kabbalist is more likely to have studied psychology and science than magic in order to connect with his or her true nature and so bring about the accomplishment of the Great Work.

This is not to deny the existence of a benign force upon which we can call for guidance, healing and divine intervention, but it is likely that all expressions of this force, from the appearance of angels to miraculous cures, are a projection of our own divine Higher Self. Evil is therefore simply the conscious denial of our true nature and the wilful refusal to see it in others. The only destructive forces on earth are the result of human behaviour and random acts of nature (some of which are exacerbated by human action). This is the reason why it appears that God does not intervene in human affairs. We are God in finite form and if we do not act to alleviate suffering when we have the power to do so, then we cannot expect a hand to reach down from the sky and put everything to rights. By believing in an omnipotent celestial being we effectively delegate responsibility to another and relinquish our right and duty to make the world a better place, which is one of the reasons for our existence.

'God', in the traditional sense, is merely another word for life in all its forms, wherever it exists in the universe. As such, God is still in a state of becoming. For we are continually evolving, and although this may often be perceived as a painful process, we will ultimately overcome our fears and doubts to manifest the divine in the universe we have created. This is the central message at the heart of contemporary Kabbalah, although it must be said that this is not a philosophy that is shared by all in the tradition.

There are many strands of the golden thread that make up the Hokhmah Nistarah (ageless wisdom), and newcomers may be confused and even put off by some of the practices that have come under the scrutiny of the media recently. For this reason it needs to be stated at the outset that the true tradition, in whatever form it is presented, does not require initiates to wear a red string around their wrist or do anything other than study the teachings and practise the exercises, which are designed to awaken the divine within and in doing so bring an understanding of our place and purpose in existence. Anything else is to be considered irrelevant.

The Four Worlds

Our physical universe is not the only reality. But it is the only reality most people are aware of, because they are constantly preoccupied with their physical needs and would not be able to function if other worlds and their inhabitants intruded into their everyday lives. However, our increasing fascination with psychic abilities and supernatural phenomena, together with the universal belief in a heavenly paradise to which our soul returns after death, suggests that the vast majority of human beings share an instinctive belief that another dimension exists beyond our normal sensory perception.

Mystics, psychics and spiritual seekers through the ages have known of the existence of these other realities and have developed techniques for exploring these dimensions at will by attaining heightened states of consciousness, some intuitively, some with the aid of hallucinogenic substances and others through spiritual disciplines, one of these being Kabbalah.

Kabbalah envisages the descent of the divine in terms of four distinct stages of creation, four interdependent and interpenetrating Worlds, each containing the essence of those from which it was generated. These are:

❖ **The World of Emanation (Azilut):** the realm of spirit or divine essence, beyond time and space, where the laws and dynamics of creation await the divine will

❖ **The World of Creation (Beriah):** the dimension of universal consciousness, inhabited by the Archangels, each personifying the quality and energy of a specific sefirah

❖ **The World of Formation (Yezirah):** the emotional realm, which psychics call the astral plane. It is this world through which we wander in our more lucid dreams and to which we return during the first stage of the transition we call death. It is the dimension where our thoughts take on temporary form, where we create our own personal heaven or hell. It is the realm described in the Old Testament as the Garden of Eden, where the 'models' for the various species were determined before incarnating in their infinite variety in the World of Action. It is also the dimension of the angelic hosts, discarnate entities who ensure that the evolutionary impulse takes the form designated by the will of God.

❖ **The World of Action (Assiyah):** our physical world

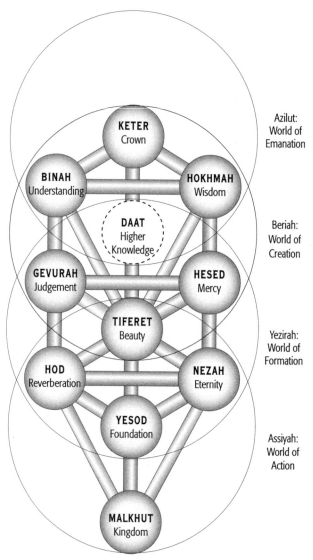

The Four Worlds

As an embodiment of the divine, we exist in the Four Worlds simultaneously, as we possess a spirit, an intellect, an emotional body and a physical form. Practical Kabbalah is therefore concerned with developing a heightened awareness of all four states and the elements within them so that we can sustain a continual sense of the upper worlds whilst exercising control over the mental and emotional dimensions and cultivating a compassionate detachment from the material world.

The process of creation is encoded in the Old Testament, where the different names for God are highly significant. For example, ELOHIM and YHVH ELOHIM are not simply random variations, but signify new stages in the process of the divine descent into matter. ELOHIM is plural and as such denotes the coming together of two attributes, whereas the composite name YHVH ELOHIM translates as God the Creator, denoting that the World of Formation emanated from the heart centre of the world above, the World of Creation.

Angels and demons

Traditional Kabbalah acknowledges the existence of angels and demons, the latter being the inhabitants of a distorted dimension resulting from a failed first attempt by the creator to form the universe, hence its name Kelippot, or the Realm of Shells (meaning shattered vessels). But modern Kabbalah considers such concepts to be an invention of the medieval mind, for the divine would not be capable of creating anything that is imperfect or evil.

Instead modern Kabbalists see angels and demons in psychological terms, as personifications of our thoughts, fears and memories, which can be projected from the unconscious in times of crisis or during altered states of consciousness such as in deep sleep or meditation. Such beings can be thought of as sub-personalities that can have an unconscious influence on our actions and impulses, compelling us to act out of character or assume an archetypal role in a certain situation. We are all capable of acting the fool, playing the victim and alternating between the saint and the sinner when it suits us. Such undeveloped or primitive aspects more commonly manifest when someone comes under the influence of drugs or alcohol, for then their dominant personality is no longer in control.

These projections of our own unconscious are not, however, to be confused with the Dibbuk, discarnate spirits of the deceased who were malevolent, pathologically disturbed or addictive personalities in life and who may seek to gratify their unnatural appetites by feeding off a living person with similar inclinations. But such mischievous entities are no danger to most of us, for the Universal Law states that 'like attracts like'. So long as you explore the spiritual path with good intentions and do not dabble with ouija boards and other dubious practices, then you are extremely unlikely to encounter anything 'evil' or unsettling. In Kabbalah there is no devil and nor is there a hell, other than that of our own making. Satan is our shadow self, the doubter who seeks to undermine our development by tempting us to indulge our baser instincts in order to test our commitment to the Great Work of Unification.

If, by any chance, you are disturbed by anything, real or imagined, all you have to do is centre yourself by performing the Tuning Up exercise (see page 40) and then ground yourself by stamping your feet and splashing your hands and face with cold water. If the feeling persists, then invoke divine protection using prayer or go for a walk, preferably in a garden or park, where nature will help to earth you and restore your sense of well-being. The same technique is also effective in clearing the residue of vivid and persistent nightmares.

Kabbalah and the angels

There is compelling and overwhelming experiential evidence to support the belief that angels can and do intervene in human affairs, although many modern Kabbalists are inclined to believe that the vast majority of these experiences involve a projection of the individual's Higher (or true) Self. During the course of writing a book on the subject of angels, I was privileged to be granted an interview with Z'ev ben Shimon Halevi, one of the world's leading authorities on the Kabbalah and the author of several definitive books on the subject. The following is a brief extract from the interview, in which Halevi defines the nature of angels and the purpose of their existence according to Kabbalistic teaching:

> *In the Kabbalistic tradition, the Archangels and the lesser angels are distinct discarnate entities confined to the upper worlds of Creation (Beriah) and Formation (Yezirah) respectively. They are personifications of the divine attributes and creative principles in their respective worlds, marshalled under the Archangel Michael. The Archangels are responsible for the grand design of the universe, from the smallest particle to human DNA, while the lesser angels oversee every process. We have given them wings to signify that they are not of this Earth, but in reality they do not possess wings. Why would they need wings if they are not physical beings? Our perception of them has to be symbolic because their true nature is beyond our limited comprehension.*

> *We can create angelic thought forms through intense meditation, but we are of an entirely different order from the celestial angelics. We have the capacity to experience the higher realms through meditation, but the angels cannot move outside their world of influence*

and are not permitted to interfere in our world. The Holy One is like a parent who knows that it is better to let its offspring learn by their mistakes, through experience, rather than continually correcting them. But without human beings there would be no evolutionary process. The universe would exist for no purpose, like a theatre without actors.

Halevi discourages his pupils and readers from petitioning the angels and instead urges them to appeal directly to the divine:

Petitioning or invoking the angels is magic, and magic is forbidden by the Kabbalah. You can appeal to God, and if he decides to intervene, he will give it to the appropriate angel.

A good example of what can happen when you appeal to the angels directly is that of the young man who petitioned Venus to intervene in his love life. The next month he got all the action he wanted. He was pursued by two women, one of whom was an athletic yoga teacher, and within weeks he was burnt out, drained of vitality and fit for nothing.

On a more serious note, if you attune to an entity you can become possessed or psychologically unbalanced. We are like receivers, and if we tune into a particular frequency on which the angel or planet of our choice is operating, we could be overwhelmed by its signal, and our psychological balance could be disturbed. You can acknowledge and respect the angels, but you must not worship them.

(The full version of this interview can be found in *Contact Your Guardian Angel*, Quantum/Foulsham, 2004.)

Supplemental work: drawing the Tree

As with any abstract concept, you will find it difficult to understand the significance of the sefirotic system and to relate its principles to the 'real world' unless you transcribe it onto paper as part of a formal exercise. By writing something down you are more likely to remember it than if you merely repeat it several times. But drawing the Tree of Life is more than creating an aide memoire. If done in silent contemplation it is an act of initiation in which you demonstrate your commitment, and in so doing you will begin to appreciate the scheme, with its relationships, principles and and dynamics, at work within the Tree far more easily than if you simply commit the names and their alignment to memory.

Having drawn the basic scheme and indicated the spheres by name, you can begin to add colour, whose significance should become clear as you consider the relationship between the triads.

✤ The supernal Keter–Hokhmah–Binah triad is left white to indicate divine light.

✤ Binah–Hokhmah–Tiferet is shaded blue to symbolise the realm of spirit.

✤ The side triads are coloured purple to represent the soul.

✤ The lower triads should be in red to denote the region of flesh and blood.

Your choice of materials and the way you draw the Tree can reveal a lot about your current state of mind, your attitude to the work, your relationships and your life in general.

If you draw freehand, this suggests you are comfortable expressing yourself plainly and honestly and that you prefer reacting to planning. You are intuitive, confident that you can work things out as you go along and not afraid of making a mistake. If you choose to use a compass and ruler, this indicates a desire for structure, stability and organisation. You need to consider all your options before you commit yourself to anything and you think carefully about what you want to say before you say it. Once you have committed yourself to something, you give it your all, and you disapprove of anyone who takes a casual approach to their work and to their life in general.

Supplemental work: correspondences

Now that you have drawn the basic Tree you can begin to fill in the details, which will reveal the unity and structure behind the Kabbalistic concept of the universe. Beginning with the sefirot, add the names of the angels and the planets, then assign the Hebrew letters and the Tarot cards to the paths. If you can work this out for yourself, you will learn much more than if you simply copy it from the diagrams in this book, but at the beginning it is sufficient to make a copy, as this will impress the scheme on your unconscious mind.

Supplemental work: Jacob's Ladder

Your final drawing will depict the Four Worlds, known to initiates as Jacob's Ladder, as they are a map of ascent from our world of action to reunification with the divine. The lowest of the four interpenetrating Trees illustrates the internal structure of the human body, the second details the psychological dimension, the third is the world of spirit, and the fourth is the dimension of the divine, in which each sefirah is assigned one of the various names of God to denote that there is multiplicity even at this level.

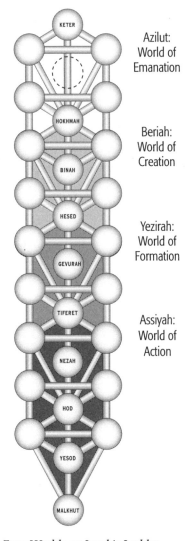

Azilut:
World of
Emanation

Beriah:
World of
Creation

Yezirah:
World of
Formation

Assiyah:
World of
Action

The Four Worlds as Jacob's Ladder

Supplemental work: the living planet

The Earth, like us, came into being as an accumulation of energy and matter at atomic and molecular levels, which became denser until it took on an appearance of solidity. But the Earth also has its layers and elements corresponding to those manifest in ourselves. It has a metallic core encased in rock, corresponding to the mineral element and skeletal component in our body; oceans covering a large proportion of its surface, which correspond to our bodily fluids; an atmosphere which is invisible but vital for life, corresponding to the air in our lungs; and it radiates an energy field suggestive of a sentient being, which corresponds to the human aura. Its surface also sustains the four stages of organic life present in our physical make-up – mineral, vegetable, animal and human.

Many students of the esoteric disciplines tend to confuse self-awareness with being self-centred and can become compulsively analytical and obsessed by psychic and psychological phenomena. What is needed instead is a balanced, detached approach in which you seek self-knowledge, not self-aggrandisement, and view yourself and everyone else on this planet as a miracle of natural evolution and the embodiment of the divine spark. You cannot walk the spiritual path as casually as you might take a stroll through the countryside. The invisible world is an extension of the natural world and operates according to the same laws. You need to understand the environment you are going to explore, otherwise you risk misinterpreting the images and impressions you receive during what will be a highly subjective experience. Remember, the lower self can distort what it sees according to its conditioning. In spiritual work ignorance is not bliss; it is positively dangerous. The better informed you are, the more you will understand when you glimpse the greater reality. So whether you are a serious student of Kabbalah or are merely exploring alternative philosophies, you should have a working knowledge of natural history.

A brief outline of how our planet came into being and how life on earth developed should be sufficient in order for you to appreciate the forces at work in the world around you. Buy or borrow a child's history of the natural world, as they generally explain the processes in simple terms and provide clear diagrams, or if you want a serious but highly entertaining scientific study, I strongly recommend *Coming of Age in the Milky Way* by Timothy Ferris (Vintage 1991). Alternatively, you could watch one of the many excellent videos and DVDs that are widely available on the subject in many languages. I recommend David Attenborough's *The Living Planet* (BBC) and *Life On Earth* (BBC) as well as *The Planets* (BBC), narrated by Samuel West.

3

Man the Microcosm

The key to all spiritual work is self-awareness, and in Kabbalah this begins with an exploration of the physical body, for unless we have a rudimentary knowledge of physiology we will be unable to understand the more abstract aspects of our being.

In Kabbalistic terms, the human body corresponds to Malkhut, the lowest point on the Tree of Life in Assiyah (the World of Action). It is the vessel in which our divine essence is grounded, and we need to become acutely aware of its structure and dynamics in order to appreciate the principles that govern ourselves and the world around us.

We are beings of pure consciousness with a psychological and emotional element that we acquired in our descent from the divine realm of Azilut (Emanation). In order to function in this physical dimension we needed a vehicle that would respond to our will, and so nature created the miracle of molecular engineering we call the human body. Unfortunately, this miracle has its drawbacks. It has a limited lifespan and its influence is restricted to the physical dimension. If you have ever had an out-of-body experience or a lucid dream, you will know the frustration of trying to connect with physical objects and seeing your hand pass through them as if you were a ghost – which is a fair definition of what you are in this non-corporeal state. Fortunately, we are able to discard our body when it becomes too frail and slip into another, a process we term reincarnation. Most of humanity is unaware of the fact that the human body has an etheric counterpart, a matrix of psychic energy that gives it finite form and to which it is connected at key points commonly known by their Sanskrit name, chakras. When there is a spiritual, mental or emotional imbalance, it can affect the free flow of etheric energy from these centres and may manifest physical symptoms to draw attention to the dis-ease within. To understand how our psychological state directly affects our physical well-being you only have to remind yourself of what happens when you are under stress. Reflexively your muscles tense, your throat tightens and your heart beats faster. Adrenaline is pumped into your system in preparation for fight or flight.

Such reactions occur unconsciously because our autonomic nervous system interfaces with our body at Yesod (ego), the point through which we perceive the world. If we could detach ourselves from sources of stress by altering our perception so as to be in the world but not of it, then we might not manifest the symptoms of stress as a result.

The same is true in reverse. If our bodies are subjected to abuse, neglect or over-indulgence, the psyche may suffer as a consequence. Excessive alcohol, the side-effects of drugs (whether prescribed or otherwise), poor diet, prolonged inactivity, stress and violence resonate at all levels, causing long-term damage not only to the body but also to the psyche. In such cases we need to exercise our will over the body in order to break the habit, for the body learns in the same way that the mind does, by conditioning.

We are grounded in the fourth of four worlds and so it is appropriate that we should manifest these four levels in finite form. For that reason, we have a solid aspect that corresponds to our bones, muscles and vital organs. We also have a fluid element in the form of our blood, enzymes, adrenaline and secretions, including sweat and tears. The element of air is present in our lungs and in our various gases, while fire exists in the form of heat generated in the skin.

To raise your awareness of these elements within, perform the following exercise once a day for a week.

Exercise: the four elements

❖ Sit with your feet flat on the floor and your legs slightly apart, parallel with your shoulders. Your arms can hang loosely by your sides or you can support your hands in your lap.

❖ Close your eyes and focus on your breath. This is the element of air, which is vital for our survival and yet most of us give it little or no thought. Take a long, deep breath and hold it for a moment. Abide in the serenity of that stillness before exhaling as slowly and fully as you can to expel every last particle of stale air from your lungs. Then re-establish your natural rhythm of breathing.

❖ When you have established a steady, relaxed rhythm, begin to sense the weight of your body in the chair. Become conscious of the frame formed by your bones and the support afforded by the skeleton. This is the solid, earthly aspect of your body. Can you attune to the beating of your heart and the rhythm of the other vital organs as they perform their critical functions? These sustain you even when you are unconscious of their existence. Consider how such processes are possible and the nature of whatever animates the human body.

❖ Next, focus on the fluid aspect of your body. Sense the circulation of the blood and the regular rhythm of your pulse. Consider how the body regulates its temperature by excreting sweat as a reflex, without any conscious effort on your behalf. Contemplate how it ensures that its needs for sustenance are met, prompting us to drink to avoid dehydration or fast to balance our metabolism. Consider, too, how the will can override the needs of the body when we over-indulge in food or drink and how this makes us feel.

❖ Finally, focus on the element of fire expressed in the heat of your skin and the radiance of etheric energy surrounding the body, known as the aura. It is this emanation of energy that is represented by the halo in religious art and it surrounds us all. Its colours reflect our spiritual development and state of mind, as well as our health. Those who have developed psychic sight (which is simply a sensitivity to the subtle energies of the non-physical world) claim to be able to see impressions of a person's previous lives in their aura. (Such sensitivity takes practice to develop, but you can prove the existence of the aura for yourself by holding your hand at arm's length against a plain surface such as a blank wall or table top and softening your gaze so that you focus on the background and not your hand. After a few moments you should be able to see a faint electric blue outline surrounding your hand. This is the first level of the aura. (For more on developing psychic sensitivity, see Chapter 9.)

❖ When you are ready, end the exercise by grounding yourself, by stamping your feet, rinsing your hands in cold water, taking a short walk in the fresh air or thinking about what you plan to do for the rest of the day.

Supplemental work: basic anatomy

You will need to supplement the practical exercises in this chapter by acquiring a basic knowledge of anatomy and physiology – but you don't have to commit yourself to an intense course. A children's introduction to anatomy should provide an adequate framework, and a week's reading should be sufficient to familiarise yourself with the main elements, as well as providing material to help in the following visualisations.

Exercise: body work

In order to raise your awareness of the connection between body and spirit and to enable you to meditate on the mechanical aspect of the body, you will need to establish a daily exercise routine based on either yoga (there is a wealth of books on yoga available in most good book shops and libraries) or tai chi. I can recommend *Step-By-Step Tai Chi* by Master Lam Kam Chuen (Gaia Books), *The Complete Book of Tai Chi Chuan* by Wong Kiew Kit (Element) and *How To Develop Chi Power* by William Cheung (O'Hara Publishing).

Between ten and twenty minutes of practice each morning and again each evening will be sufficient to attune you, and it will also provide the ideal preparation for Kabbalistic meditation or study.

During the exercise be mindful of your posture. Are you exerting too much effort? Are your movements fluid and economical? Be conscious of the circulation of air and energy and the sense of balance obtained in moments of stillness.

The upper and lower faces

Having established the concept of the Tree within, you can take the idea further by envisaging the lower part of the body below the solar plexus as corresponding to the lower face of the Tree. Here are to be found the elements of earth and water in the form of the legs and the stomach, which performs the vital function of digestion. The remaining elements of air and fire can be seen as corresponding to the lungs and the brain, in which consciousness resides.

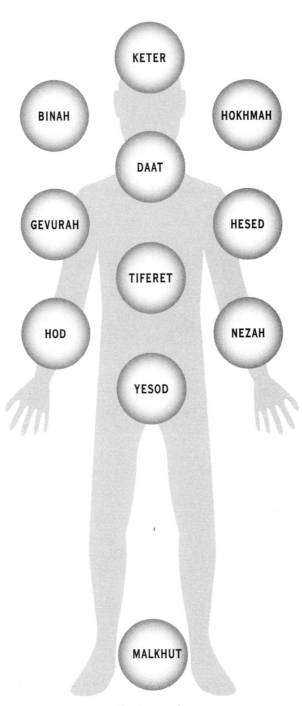

The Tree within

If you imagine superimposing the sefirot on the body, with the Crown just above your head and Malkhut between your feet, you will see that the sefirot roughly correspond to the chakras, or energy centres, of the ancient Indian tradition.

Visualising the spheres superimposed on your body and then raising your awareness of each in sequence will not only help to impress the scheme on your conscious mind but will also serve as a vital preparation ritual, making you more receptive to the subtle energies of the upper and inner worlds. If you can also visualise the colours associated with each sphere, you will be able to stimulate the corresponding chakra at each level, which will ensure the free flow of psychic energy around the body, leaving you feeling energised, alert and positive for the day ahead. For this reason I suggest you do the following exercise every morning on waking.

Exercise: tuning up

You can perform this exercise either mentally or physically, touching each sphere in turn with the right palm and ending with the hands over the head, palms upward, in a gesture indicating a willingness to receive the divine blessing.

❖ Stand with your feet slightly apart and your arms resting by your sides.

❖ Close your eyes and begin by visualising yourself standing on a rustic brown sphere that pulses with the energy of the Earth. This sphere is the manifestation of Malkhut (Kingdom) which is the grounding point and your source of vital physical energy.

❖ Now raise you awareness to the area below your navel and envisage a red sphere corresponding to Yesod (Foundation), from which you derive your sense of identity.

❖ To either side of your hips are Hod (Reverberation/Intellect) and Nezah (Eternity/Instinct), the spheres of action, the former providing the passive link to the lower half of the body and the latter providing the active link. Both can be visualised as orange in colour.

❖ The sphere of Tiferet (Beauty) lies over the solar plexus and is traditionally envisaged as being yellow. This is the sphere associated with the Higher Self and is the emotional centre of the psyche, which equates with the stomach and digestion on the physical level. For this reason emotional upsets and inability to express your emotions can manifest as nervous stomach disorders, indigestion and, in extreme cases, stomach ulcers. To avoid such problems you need to process your emotions as efficiently as you digest your food.

✤ To either side of the heart are Gevurah (Judgement) and Hesed (Mercy), which relate to the heart chakra, in the centre of the chest. They are both envisaged as green, which is the colour of harmony and of the meeting point of the natural and supernatural worlds. The heart centre and the corresponding spheres can be seen as the point at which we ideally temper justice with compassion and reach decisions after considering the consequences.

✤ Daat, the unmanifest attribute representing Higher Knowledge, can be envisaged as a soft blue sphere over the throat and face, governing sensory input and self-expression. Here, again, the four elements find expression, with the eyes being organs of light, the ears and nose being organs of air, the tongue being the organ of water, and the body as a whole representing the earth.

✤ To either side of the head are the spheres of Binah (Understanding) and Hokhmah (Wisdom), which can be envisaged as violet and purple respectively.

✤ The final sephirah is Keter (Crown), above the head, which can be visualised as a blinding white sphere.

Note: If you have been studying basic anatomy as suggested, you will note that the pelvic cavity corresponds to the triads comprising Yesod, Hod, Nezah and Tiferet, while the chest cavity corresponds to Gevurah, Hesed and Tiferet.

Exercise: self-analysis using the sefirot

You can either do this exercise with a pen and paper or simply sit quietly and work through it mentally.

❖ Beginning with Malkhut, centre yourself in the physical world by listing all the physical activities you do during a typical day.

❖ Now rise to Yesod and itemise all the personal contacts you had today and how these affected your moods and your perception of yourself. How did you act with and react to those you came into contact with?

❖ Next raise your awareness to Hod by recalling your favourite books and why they appeal to you. Think, too, about the way you express yourself in writing and any other forms of communication you use to convey your feelings, attitudes and ideas. Do you prefer to sit down and write a letter so that you can consider your words carefully, or do you feel more comfortable talking face to face? Maybe you prefer to talk on the phone. If so, why do you choose this method of communication? Is it so that you can say things you would be uncomfortable expressing face to face, or do you need to be able to talk without interruption? Are you really listening to the other person or just waiting for a chance to continue your monologue?

❖ Now raise your awareness to Nezah, the sphere of sensuality. Are you comfortable with your sexuality? Do you consider yourself self-assured or self-conscious? Do you hide behind false modesty or are you brash and forthright? Are you intolerant of those who are overtly self-possessed? Do you act on impulse or do you fear that you may do something foolish or spend too much and find yourself in financial difficulties? Do you need to justify all your actions to yourself? Do you live in fear of becoming ill, or are you too involved in life-enhancing activities to consider the possibility?

❖ Next rise to Tiferet by asking yourself who you really are. How would you describe the true you? We act according to whose company we are in and the role we are expected to play, but who are you when you are alone and doing what gives you the greatest pleasure and fulfilment?

❖ Now ascend to Gevurah by considering how you arrive at decisions. Do you find it difficult to make decisions because of the necessity to appease or consider the views and needs of others? Are you overly critical of yourself and others or would you consider yourself to be tolerant and even-tempered? Do you need to be in control of events and your emotions, or would you describe yourself as easy-going? Do you need to be 'right' all the time, or do you readily admit when you are wrong? Are you willing to learn from others?

❖ Rising to Hesed, consider how compassionate and considerate you are. Are you too soft and too ready to forgive? Do others take advantage of your good nature? Are there occasions when you deliberately 'rescue' others so that you can feel righteous and spiritually superior? Is someone in your life playing the victim and do you encourage their dependency by acting as their rescuer? Can you allow your friends and family to learn by their own mistakes or are you constantly trying to save them from themselves? Can you forgive those who have hurt or offended you?

❖ Now rise to Binah by recalling a time when you intuitively knew how to do something you hadn't learnt or previously even thought about. Where did that knowledge come from?

❖ You now come to Daat, the abyss or the Veil of Hidden Knowledge, as it is sometimes called. Close your eyes and sit in silence for a few moments. How does that make you feel? What thoughts go through your mind? Are you comfortable in the dark or anxious? Do you feel guilty sitting and doing nothing or do you welcome the opportunity to sit in silence? Are you restless and eager to return to an activity? Do you feel vulnerable in the dark, or strong and secure within yourself?

✤ Now cross to Hokhmah and recall a time when you were inspired to do or create something. Perhaps you surprised yourself by offering a piece of wise advice to a friend or family member that revealed the truth of a situation. Or maybe you saw to the heart of a matter that was causing difficulties for you and in so doing enabled the problem naturally to resolve itself.

✤ Finally, ascend to Keter by visualising a brilliant sphere of white light over your head and surrender to the Higher Will that this light represents.

✤ When you are ready, return to waking consciousness. Consider the insights you have gleaned from this exercise and how you can put your new understanding into practice.

4

Secrets of the Scriptures

Judaism is not alone in perpetuating practices the meaning of which has long been lost on both the priests and their congregation. All religions have an exoteric (outer) and an esoteric (inner) aspect, the former being the rituals, customs and festivals that offer its members both continuity and a sense of community, but which in time become empty and meaningless unless their origin and significance are understood. Without an understanding of the principles on which the rites and laws are based, the community is acting in blind faith and a sense of duty to its ancestors. It is seeing only the surface reflection and not the substance of the teaching on which its faith was founded.

Due to the distrust with which orthodox Judaism has viewed Kabbalah because of its association with magic, the majority of both orthodox and liberal Jews are unaware of basic Kabbalistic principles and cosmology. Few are aware that every aspect of Jewish religious life is an expression of the Kabbalistic concept of existence, from the design of the synagogue and the layered vestments of the Rabbis to the ritual objects used in worship. For example, the seven-armed candlestick known as the Menorah is fashioned from one single piece of metal to symbolise the unity of the divine World of Emanation. The outer arms represent the pillars of Severity and Mercy, while the central axis corresponds to the pillar of Equilibrium. Its base represents Malkhut, and the joints on the central axis in order of ascent represent the corresponding spheres of Yesod, Tiferet and Daat. The seven candle holders represent the remaining sefirot, while the arms and the spaces in between correspond to the Four Worlds.

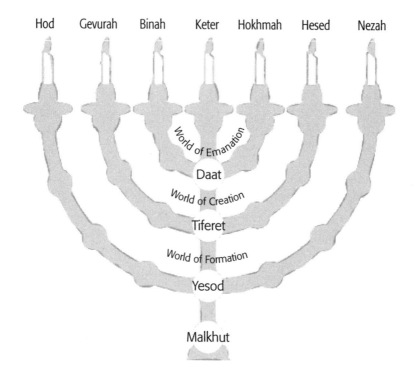

Hod   Gevurah   Binah   Keter   Hokhmah   Hesed   Nezah

World of Emanation

Daat

World of Creation

Tiferet

World of Formation

Yesod

Malkhut

Menorah and the Four Worlds

Kabbalah and the Bible

For the Kabbalist, the Bible is much more than a history of the Jewish people. It is an allegory of the human condition and a detailed description of everyman's descent from, and return to, the divine. It was intended to be read and understood on several levels – literal, allegorical and metaphysical – each stage corresponding to an awakening of one of the three triads on the Tree.

It is not necessary for the modern Kabbalist to study the Torah as intensively as their predecessors would have done, but this scripture remains a rich source of wisdom and spiritual knowledge that should at least be understood in principle.

The Ten Commandments

The Ten Commandments, for example, can be taken literally as an ethical code for righteous living or metaphorically as a guide for self-realisation. Each Commandment refers to specific sefirot, the first three corresponding to the spheres of the divine triad; the fourth and fifth emphasising the importance of devotion and respect for one's parents and for the Sabbath; the remainder relating to good practice. In this context the edict forbidding murder is referring to destruction not in the physical but in the spiritual sense, as by committing murder (or suicide) we deny our divine nature and limit our potential (personified by Tiferet). Adultery relates to the negative aspect of Nezah, which expresses itself in self-aggrandisement, and theft can be read as the wilful misuse of knowledge (Hod) to gain unfair advantage over others.

Bearing false witness is understood to equate with acknowledging the dangers of self-delusion, and the Commandment forbidding the coveting of another person's position or possessions is a warning against unchecked desire – a reminder that we all have our path to follow and our own share of blessings and trials. It is self-defeating and unproductive to compare our life with that of our neighbour.

Exodus

In the Bible, 'Israel' does not refer to a specific state or race, but to humankind. Therefore the reference to the 12 tribes of Israel in the Book of Exodus is considered by Kabbalists to be an allusion to the 12 basic human archetypes, and their story to be an allegory of the evolution of the human individual.

The enslavement of the Israelites by the Egyptians may have been a historical fact, but the reason for its inclusion in Exodus is to illustrate the necessity for reincarnation. It is no coincidence that the Hebrew word for Egypt (Mizraim) translates as 'confined', nor is Jacob's coat of many colours a mere fanciful detail of the storyteller's imagination. The Kabbalist interprets the coat as being the radiant aura surrounding the body and Joseph's dreams as the human capacity for glimpsing the greater reality that exists beyond the mundane and material world.

In the esoteric tradition, the story of Moses and his freeing of the Hebrew slaves is another example of allegory. Having fled Egypt (which represents ordinary consciousness), Moses is reluctant to return but eventually relents, knowing the importance of initiating others so that they too can be liberated from bondage. But first he must overcome Pharaoh, who symbolises temporal power. Moses does this by transforming his staff into a snake, which then devours the serpents conjured by Pharaoh's magicians. In this he demonstrates that miracles are superior to magic, in other words that the will of God is greater than the will of the senses or that the will of the Higher Self is superior to that of the ego.

Even after this setback Pharaoh does not relent, refusing to accept the inevitable, which can be interpreted as the reluctance of the individual to acknowledge the need for change. But as with Pharaoh, if we continue to resist we will soon be forced to face reality by the onset of a crisis of our own making.

In the Old Testament this crisis is symbolised by the ten plagues, which equate with the vices that are the reverse of the divine attributes of the sefirot. Moses and his brother Aaron invoke the plagues in four stages, in a reversal of the unfolding of the Four Worlds, Moses dealing with those concerned with fire and air, and Aaron with those corresponding to earth and water, with God or nature visiting the remainder upon the Egyptians.

Having finally secured the release of the Israelites, Moses leads them to freedom, parting the Red Sea, which is symbolic of commitment to the spiritual path, the point of no return. From here they travel across the desert and endure privation and doubt, the arid desert and unforgiving sun being symbolic of the no man's land between sensual indulgence and the promised land of spiritual awakening.

Jesus – master Kabbalist

Joshua ben Miriam has been mythologised by orthodox Christianity as the one and only son of God who was sent to Earth to save sinners from themselves.

However, according to Kabbalistic teachings we are all divine in essence and capable of attaining a heightened level of awareness equating with Tiferet, known as the seat of Solomon or, in Christian occultism, as the Christ consciousness. It is quite probable that Jesus was the anointed one, the Messiah, the most fully realised human being on Earth and the axis of his age; he was certainly a maggid (or teacher) and a master of Kabbalah.

It is believed that his mission was to raise the consciousness of humanity by first making people aware that the Kingdom of Heaven (the Malkhut of Azilut or Foundation of the Divine World) was within them and not a reward awaiting them in paradise if they obeyed the will of the high priests. The first step on Jacob's ladder lies within us all. When Jesus spoke of no-one being allowed to come before God unless they came through him, he was not demanding obedience or worship for himself, but was referring to his role as the embodiment of Tiferet, the Higher Self. He was stating the simple fact that if we want to return to the source, we too must undertake the journey to realisation and pass through this point. No-one, not even the Messiah, can do this for us.

This is the message encoded in the Lord's Prayer, whose wording (in the original Aramaic) corresponds to the sefirot on the Tree of Life. By asking his followers to take this invocation to their hearts, Jesus was ensuring that it would ultimately awaken and transform those who repeated it as they eventually became aware of its spiritual significance.

The Kabbalistic cross

It is not widely known that the cross was a central symbol for the early Kabbalists long before the birth of Jesus. The vertical line represented the aspirational impulse and the horizontal axis symbolised the physical plane. The arms of the cross represented the Four Worlds, the four elements within, the four cardinal points of the universe and the four Archangels. It is thought that this original mystical significance was the reason why the cross was belatedly adopted as the symbol of the new sect in preference to the Chi-Rho emblem, which they had used in the years after the crucifixion.

As an initiate of the Nazarenes and a practising Kabbalist, Jesus would have been familiar with the occult significance of the cross, a belief confirmed by the inclusion of Kabbalistic principles in the Lord's Prayer (see above).

Invoking the cross establishes a connection with the Christ consciousness at Tiferet and serves as an effective method for closing down at the end of a session or for invoking protection.

Exercise: the Kabbalistic cross

❖ Stand with your arms loosely by your sides and visualise a sphere of white light above the crown of your head. Sense its radiance and the life force pulsing within it as you begin to draw it down through your head and into your body to activate the energy centres aligned along the spinal column.

❖ Place the finger tips of both your hands together before you, as in prayer, to symbolise the unity of the ten sefirah.

❖ Touch the middle of your forehead with the tips of your right hand as you say the Hebrew word ATEH (thine is).

❖ Using the same hand, touch your heart centre while visualising drawing the light down in one fluid motion from the brow to the heart and say MALKUTH (the kingdom).

❖ Touch your right shoulder while visualising drawing the light from the heart to the shoulder and say VEGEVURAH (and the power) and across to the left shoulder intoning VEGEDULAH (and the glory).

❖ Finally, bring both palms together again as in prayer, with your thumbs pointing to your chest, and say LE OLAM OMAIN (forever, amen).

Note: In this context the heart, and not the feet, is used to denote the grounding centre (Malkhut).

5

Tree of the Psyche

I n this chapter we will be exploring the relationship between the psyche and the body, looking at how the sefirot of the psychological Tree resonate in the lower physical realm to manifest as particular behaviour – or, in extreme cases, as disorders or dis-ease.

Personal consciousness

In the Tree of the psyche, the sphere of Yesod corresponds to ordinary consciousness, which is our natural waking state. Freud called this self-centred aspect of our personality the ego, and as such it has acquired a negative connotation that gives a false impression of its true nature, which is to act as the window through which we view the world and our relationship to it.

But Yesod has two facets, perception of reality and its opposite attribute – imagination. This is possible because at this point the Tree of the psyche interfaces with the Tree of the body, giving Yesod a connection with Daat, the unmanifest attribute representing Hidden Knowledge. This relationship between the spheres in interconnecting dimensions can provide infinite insights for the student who wishes to understand how this interaction operates in the higher worlds, but for present purposes it is sufficient for you to understand that neither Tree should be seen as a two-dimensional diagram, but rather as a portal into other realities, like a wormhole connecting alternative universes. Just remember that the Yesod of one tree does not correspond with the Yesod of the next, but instead interfaces at Tiferet. The base of the higher tree is always rooted in the heart of the one beneath it.

Using your imagination as a vehicle for consciousness, you can raise or lower your awareness of the upper or lower worlds through the Yesod–Tiferet portal in a guided visualisation such as the one on page 52. By this means you can, for example, become aware of the generally unnoticed processes of your body so that you can avoid illness before it manifests.

Exercise: the seed

This is a physical exercise that should be performed on a bed or mat. If this is difficult for you to do or you feel self-conscious, you can do the exercise as a visualisation. However, it should be understood that physical activity leaves a deeper impression on the psyche and so is more effective.

✤ Curl yourself into a ball with your knees tucked into your chest and your arms folded across your chest.

✤ Begin by visualising yourself as a small seed deep within which can be sensed the germ of life waiting upon favourable conditions to begin the growth process. All the nutritional material you need to awaken from the dormant state is present.

✤ Now the rain falls on the surface of the soil, drumming on the roof of the darkness that surrounds you. Moisture begins to penetrate your skin and filters down to your core, activating proteins and bringing the first stirrings of life. You slowly begin to uncurl, until you are resting on your knees with your head and arms still tucked protectively into your chest.

✤ Now feel the warmth of the sun on your back as you break the surface of the soil and begin to stretch slowly upwards towards the source of life – the light.

✤ Feel the blood surging though your veins like sap rising through the seedling as you stretch your limbs like branches towards the sun and send down roots to secure you into the earth. Sense the regenerative power of the sun revitalising every cell until you are at full stretch. Then bask in the life force as you wait for nature to create ideal conditions for fertilisation so that you can bear fruit and propagate your species across the planet.

✤ Know that this organic consciousness is alive within you as the vegetable element of your being. It is this, and not your animal nature, that provides the instinctive drive to make a home, find a mate and raise a family.

✤ When you are ready, return to waking consciousness.

Animal, vegetable, mineral

We all operate on all four levels of the natural world: human, animal, vegetable and mineral. For example, when we feel too apathetic to act or express an opinion, or we avoid commitment, we are operating at the mineral level. When we care only about our own comfort, resist change and act as a passive observer, we are operating at the vegetable level. When we are competitive, cunning, social, self-preserving, courageous and in pursuit of power, we are operating at the animal level. To be truly human, however, we need to rise above all these levels and assert our individuality by focusing on our compassion, our desire for truth, our spiritual aspiration and our self-awareness. You can awaken your human attributes by reflecting on your progress so far, considering a solution to a particular problem or simply counting your blessings.

Exercise: the animal

This exercise will enable you to examine your relationship with the animal in you. Like the previous exercise, it is physical; however, if you are unable to act out the instructions or feel self-conscious, you can do the exercise as a visualisation.

✤ Begin by crouching on all fours with your eyes closed. Be perfectly still and breathe deeply. You are an animal. What animal are you? Choose the first thing that comes into your mind, as this has a symbolic significance. (If the significance of your animal is not immediately apparent, you can consult a dictionary of symbols when the exercise is complete.)

✤ Now visualise yourself in your natural environment. It is daybreak and you are alert and hungry. But you also have to feed your offspring. Do you lead them out in search of food or do you leave them behind with your mate, who will guard them while you hunt or scavenge for whatever you can find?

✤ What sensations do you experience as you exercise your animal instincts? How does it feel to exercise your animal agility and to be acutely alert to the sights and sounds of the natural world?

✤ During your search you come upon an interesting object. Your curiosity is aroused. What is it?

✤ While you are examining the object, you are challenged by another animal who senses you are intruding on its territory. What is that other animal and how do you react? Do you flee or make a show of strength? What cunning do you display?

✤ You overcome this challenge and continue your search. If you are a carnivore you may have to hunt and kill your prey. You have no pity, no feelings of any kind, only the instinct for survival. Once you have caught and killed your food you return with it to feed your mate and your offspring. Then you play with them, chasing, tumbling and teaching them by example how to hunt. If you are a herbivore, you may have to risk becoming another animal's dinner as you graze or gather your food. Do you travel with a herd for protection? Are you part of a family group? Or do you forage alone?

✤ Begin to return to human awareness, knowing that these animal instincts are alive within you. It is this animal element in us that provides the instinctive drive to conform to certain behavioural patterns and that discourages our efforts to assert our individuality.

The animal can also cause us to strike out instinctively rather than reason or reflect. You do not need to be wary of this aspect of your nature, nor should you deny it. Be conscious of it, but not prey to it.

❖ When you are ready, return to waking consciousness.

Exercise: the scrapbook

This exercise will enable you to become aware of your unique, human attributes – your capacity for reflection, recollection, reasoning, aspiration and imagination.

❖ Begin by closing your eyes and focusing on your breath.

❖ Imagine you are looking down at a scrapbook resting on your lap. It is a pictorial record of your life. What condition is it in? Is it well cared for or dusty, tatty and discoloured? Is it a slim volume or a thick book bulging with lovingly preserved items?

❖ Are you eager to look inside or reluctant? When you do open it, is it at the first page or do you let it fall open at random?

❖ Are the contents neatly arranged in chronological order and annotated or have they been dropped in loose simply to keep them under one cover?

❖ Your attitude to your past can be very revealing, but leave the analysis until later. Spend some minutes leafing through the pages at leisure. There are photographs, drawings, letters and mementos of past times, happy and otherwise. What are your most vivid memories? Can you recall them with total sensory perception? Take yourself back to a specific incident or moment and re-experience the sights, sounds, smells, touch and taste of that time.

❖ Which experiences have affected your present attitude and behaviour the most? Do you have a sense of having lost something, and, if so, has that coloured the way you look at life? What were the consequences of your most significant decisions?

❖ What ambitions did you have when you were younger and what feelings and thoughts do these awaken in you now? Do you have any regrets or residual resentment? If so, can you let them go? Can you view your past mistakes dispassionately, seeing them as necessary experiences from which you have learnt and grown?

❖ Finally, turn to the blank pages at the back, which are reserved for snapshots and souvenirs from the future. What would you like to see there when you open the book in a year from now? What would you like to see five years from now?

❖ When you are ready, return to waking consciousness and stamp your feet to ground yourself.

Taming the inner child

In recent years it has become fashionable to refer to the lower self (or ego, to use Freud's term) as the inner child and to the Higher Self (or superego) as the parental aspect of our psyche. Such terms imply that the former is by nature immature, self-centred in the negative sense and capable of distorting our perspective of the world and other people for its own self-interest. All of which is true to a degree but ignores the fact that the lower self serves a vital function and that without it we cannot achieve self-realisation or wholeness.

An important part of Kabbalastic practice therefore involves keeping the ego under constant supervision and restraint whilst acknowledging that, like a child, it is born innocent, its nature to be determined by circumstances and conditioning. Unfortunately, the more pressure that is exerted upon it, the more distorted will be its view of reality. In practice this means that if we identify exclusively with the lower self we will be dependent on other people for approval and will be likely to develop neurosis when we come under extreme stress, as pressure magnifies any flaws until our view of reality is so distorted that it becomes disturbing.

Even if you consider yourself well balanced, you need to be aware that if you undertake any spiritual work the ego will still distort your perception to a degree, interpreting the experience according to its own values and expectations. You will also need to be aware that from an early age the lower self will have developed strategies for dealing with challenging situations that can be useful in daily life but that are self-defeating in spiritual work. For example, we develop self-defence tactics that can prevent us from being open and honest in analysis or from confronting our deepest feelings. The lower self will continue to be active even after you have committed yourself to spiritual work or self-development. You need to be alert for those moments when it will try to persuade you that you do not need to grow or become self-aware, that you are perfect as you are and that all self-help is New Age nonsense. When meditating you will be plagued by nagging doubts as to the value of such practices and reminders that there are more urgent chores to be done.

To overcome the inner child's restlessness, set aside a specific time each day to practise meditation or study, and stick to it. Another strategy is to engage in mundane physical work such as digging the garden or housework in order to demonstrate to your lower self that you are not above such work. Alternatively, you could do charity work, serving in a thrift shop one afternoon a week, for example, or offer to weed an elderly neighbour's garden – all of which force the wilful inner child to submit to the superior will of the inner parent, which is capable of thinking of other people's needs and not only of its own.

If you think you are capable of being open and honest with yourself, you could try to engage the ego in a discussion with the Higher Self by writing down your aspirations, anxieties and fantasies and then allowing your unconscious to respond by recording whatever thoughts come spontaneously to mind. Try not to analyse your answers until you bring the session to an end otherwise you risk interrupting the flow. Remember, Yesod is like a wilful child who will dominate your life if you let it. It is resistant to change on principle, but it can also be conditioned, just as you were taught to fear or favour certain things by your parents and teachers. Now you have to be the parent and teacher, conditioning your inner child to do what is best for its development in the long term.

The Tree within

To understand how the Tree of the psyche and the Tree of the body interrelate and resonate on a practical level, sit still and sense the unity of your body and your complete control over it. Consider your limbs as the left and right pillars, which in turn represent the governing principles of energy and matter, active and passive, male and female. Note how these manifest in you, with one side being more dominant and the other more passive. For example, you may write with your right hand while the left offers balance, supporting your weight as you lean over the paper, holding it steady. But although one side is predominantly active and the other passive, we can only function efficiently when we attain equilibrium. The same is true on the psychological level, for without understanding, for example, we could accumulate an impressive amount of facts but have no insight into what we had learnt. The same applies to the way in which we interact with others. For example, the most constructive relationships are those in which there is a roughly equal distribution of labour and parity on other levels. This principle applies whether the relationship is within the family, or between lovers, friends or even business partners.

This constant struggle for equilibrium, for the synthesis of our complementary attributes, is the primary aim of practical Kabbalah.

Exercise: self-observation

In Kabbalah, self-awareness is valued more highly than psychic experience or even the most profound insights into the meaning of life and the nature of existence, because unless you are a fully integrated personality you risk distorting your perception of the upper worlds. To assist the process of self-awareness you could discuss your neuroses with a professional psychotherapist over the course of a year or two at great expense, or you could simply observe and reflect upon your feelings, attitudes and behaviour at key points throughout the day until you become acutely conscious of your own reflexes and responses.

Doing so will enable you to detect the subtle patterns of your life, of which you may previously have been unaware, and then to judge when it is advantageous to take certain actions and when to conserve your strength. In time you will also acquire the ability to detect subtle signs in other people's behaviour so that you will be prepared for their reaction before it can develop into a disagreement.

Exercise: predict the news before it happens

Evil appears to be predominant at the present time only because it exerts a dramatic effect on external events, whereas benign individuals exert a more subtle influence on the inner life of the individual and society.

To test the validity of this theory make a point of reading a serious newspaper every day and listening to informed opinion on radio and TV current affairs programmes so that you can begin to predict events and trends. As your sensitivity to the pattern of world events sharpens, you will be able to identify the dynamics of specific triads on the Tree at work in the world at large as communities and nations come under the influence of specific aspects of their collective personality.

✤ See if you can identify what stage of personal development a nation is expressing in its behaviour towards its neighbours – the child, adolescent, adult or elder. Can you visualise how it might improve its situation or resolve a particular difficulty if it acted in a different way?

✤ Select an individual in the news and analyse their actions using the attributes and principles of the Tree. For example, if they are intolerant of others they will be expressing the critical aspect of Gevurah (Judgement), whereas if they manifest compassion they will be expressing its complementary sefirah Hesed (Mercy).

Your mirror image

Another alternative to investing in psychoanalysis or counselling can be found close to home. Your choice of partner reveals a lot about the person you are, your self-image, the choices you have made and where you are going from here. Only in the give and take of an intimate relationship can we grow and truly come to know ourselves. Kabbalah should be practised only by those who are prepared to be tested by life and not by those who wish to escape responsibility in an idyllic spiritual retreat. After all, almost anyone can find peace of mind if they are allowed to take a break from real life. That is no true test of character.

Task: see yourself through others

If you want to understand yourself, study how you interact with other people.

❖ First consider how you relate to your most intimate companions, noting your responses and reactions throughout the day. Record any observations they make about you, but be aware that they, too, can project their own prejudices and anxieties onto you, which you should be able to identify and dismiss as such.

❖ When you feel that you have exhausted all avenues in this relationship, you can extend your study to your family and closest friends. Can you identify one person who personifies a specific characteristic that you possess? How do you react when they are with you? If it is a negative trait, are you embarrassed, defensive or threatened? Do they make you aware that you occasionally behave in this way, and, if so, can you now summon up the willpower to control it? If it is a positive characteristic, do you admire them for it, and, if so, can you now express this quality without feeling self-conscious or denying it out of a sense of false modesty?

❖ Once you can see yourself in others, the next step is to see yourself as others see you. How would you describe yourself in terms of an archetype? What single characteristic do you display in certain company? What is your role in these relationships? What functions to you perform? And which characteristics do you restrain and for what reason?

❖ Now consider how your enemies see you. Can you think of a word or phrase that they would use to describe you?

❖ Do you see any contradictions in the way that different people see you? Perhaps your partner criticises you for being inconsiderate and selfish when you express a desire to socialise with your friends, while your friends may think of you as being too easy-going and readily influenced by a stronger personality when you put them off to appease your partner. Or perhaps your partner undermines your confidence by questioning your competence and intelligence, so distorting your image of yourself. In reality, your partner is expressing their own lack of confidence, which they feel the need to prove by exercising control over an affable character who wishes to please everyone and avoid conflict at all costs.

❖ Do you see yourself cast in any of the roles described above? What other roles are you cast in?

Fate and free will

It is a common fallacy that we have achieved certain things and met certain people because fate ordained that it should be so. In contrast, Kabbalah states that free will determines the course of our lives and makes specific events inevitable. Our destiny is determined by our actions, and its course can be altered at will. The purpose of Kabbalah is to help us to become aware of the course we have embarked upon and the strength of the current so that we can capitalise on favourable conditions or batten down the hatches to ride out a storm. Suffering is not visited upon us by a cruel creator, but is often caused by our resistance to change. We fear change and seek security in the familiar, but without change we cease to grow, so unconsciously we create a crisis in order to test our integrity and commitment or to correct our wrong conduct.

Exercise: crisis

❖ Think back to a crisis you have experienced recently and consider it from your present perspective. Can you see now that it was a highly productive period in your life? It is during such times that we make the greatest progress. It is important to be aware of and to acknowledge this development.

❖ Now recall a past relationship. Remember the time when you entered it. What did you bring to it? What did your partner contribute? Now recall the relationship's end. Identify what purpose that relationship may have served.

✤ Finally, turn your attention to your friends and family. Have they ever experienced a difficult time? If so, can you identify what were the circumstances that created it and for what purpose?

The importance of a balanced personality

If one or more of the divine attributes symbolised by the sefirot are continually accentuated or developed at the expense of their complementary characteristics, a psychological imbalance can be created. In extreme cases, this may manifest as an obsession or neurosis.

Taking the lower sefirah first, people who exist entirely in Malkhut will be concerned exclusively with material possessions and obsessed with their physical appearance. If a sense of Malkhut is balanced with the other sefirot in the lower triad, Malkhut will instead keep them grounded and make them practical and pragmatic.

Those who are centred entirely in Yesod will be oblivious to the inner voice of their Higher Self. Such a person will therefore be self-centred, in the negative sense of the phrase. Such people demand constant praise from others in order to assuage their insecurity, thus revealing that they have not developed beyond the child in psychological terms.

In contrast, a person who has over-emphasised their intellect (Hod) may become an accomplished academic or scientist, but without the balance of Nezah, the intuitive aspect of the psyche, they will not develop the understanding needed to appreciate the human factor and wider consequences of their work. An example is the blinkered physicist who is so immersed in their research that they are oblivious to the use that it could be put to by the unscrupulous. Another example of the unbalanced Hodian personality is the manipulative schemer, who is likely to have little consideration for others if he or she also happens to be ego-centred, as is often the case.

We are probably all familiar with the over-indulgent Nezahian personality who gratifies their sexual and other appetites to excess and in so doing is likely to become desensitised, eventually demanding increasingly extreme stimulation as their senses become satiated.

Ascending the central column on the Tree, we come next to Tiferet, the Higher Self, at the point traditionally known as the Seat of Solomon, or, in New Age parlance, the Christ consciousness. Even a person centred in such an exalted position of heightened awareness needs the balance of the lower sphere of Yesod, for without it they will not be able to understand the needs and fallibility of their fellow humans. Such people litter the wayside on the path to enlightenment. They are the fake gurus, cult leaders and mad messiahs whose patina of charisma attracts adoring acolytes but who have allowed themselves to fall prey to the addictive power of adulation (Nezah) and the illusion of intellectual superiority (Hod).

Such self-deception often leads to a lack of judgement and compassion, such as is exhibited when Gevurah and Hesed are out of alignment. Then we see the overly critical individual who makes no allowances for his mistakes or those of other people. Nothing is good enough for the unchecked Gevurah personality, and justice in their world means severe punishment with no allowances made for mitigating circumstances. In contrast, the excessively compassionate Hesed personality allows everyone to take advantage of their forgiving nature. They also lack drive and determination and can be crippled by indecision. However, when these two attributes are in equilibrium, a person will exhibit self-discipline and discernment.

Contrary to popular belief, Wisdom (Binah) and Understanding (Hokhmah) are not the same. Wisdom comes with experience, while understanding is the result of insight. We cannot obtain either one without the other.

It needs to be understood that whilst it is natural to emphasise one aspect of our personality in accordance with our abilities or to suit a specific situation, excessive development of one attribute is likely to corrupt the adjacent ones, turning virtues into vices and, to compound the problem, unbalancing the triad.

The group mind

We pride ourselves on being individuals, but it is possible for all but the most fiercely independent-minded individual to be swept up in a tide of emotion and become part of a group mind, if only for a moment. We see this demonstrated at sports events and rock concerts when a crowd reacts as one, as well as during times of national grief and – less admirably – in the mentality of the mob and fanatical religious cults. At such times people can be compared to a herd of animals who instinctively wheel and arc as one, without a sound or sign to direct them.

Beyond our social animal instincts, we also come together on a psychological level when we unconsciously project our strengths and failings into the larger group mind we call society. Every group, from a family unit to an entire nation, creates a group mind. It is for this reason that groups can be directed to act under the will of a strong-minded, charismatic individual, as in times of war or when directed to project their prejudices onto a specific group who will act as a scapegoat to exorcise a collective anxiety. On these occasions, the leader will assume the role of the mother or father of the community or nation (at the level of Keter).

Unfortunately, it is invariably the aggressive male aspects of the group that are exploited, rarely the passive female ones. The notable exceptions have been Mahatma Ghandi, whose passive revolution forced the English out of India; President John F. Kennedy and Israeli Prime Minister Yitzhak Rabin, both of whom were assassinated; and, more recently, Diana, Princess of Wales. Her death touched long neglected female qualities in the British population, many of whom were confounded by their own feelings because they had been neglected for so long.

The growth of the individual can also be mapped out in terms of an ascent through the Tree. Malkhut represents infancy, in which we are preoccupied with physical growth, nourishment and sense perception, but have yet to develop a sense of self or of the world. As we reach childhood, we graduate to Yesod, developing an ego and becoming acutely aware of our wants and needs. Unless we have an abnormal childhood, we will learn that we are the centre of our parents' universe, and in doing so rise to Hod as a youth, learning to reason, rationalise, and determine what is in our interest and how to acquire it. We will also become sexually aware, through intimate relationships hoping to attain a degree of self-awareness equivalent to Tiferet. At this stage in our development we have the opportunity to mature and awaken the spheres of the soul triad – or oscillate, as most people do, between the lower sephirot, gratifying the senses (Nezah), attempting to exercise control over others (Hod), indulging the ego (Yesod) and acquiring possessions (Malkhut).

The reason why some people do not rise above the lower triad is that they either lack the imagination or they undermine their own efforts by building their ambitions on insecure foundations. Unless the lower spheres are sufficiently developed, they will not sustain the pressure placed upon them when the ascent is made. In other words, there is no shortcut to the top of the Tree of Life. Willpower, good looks and a persuasive personality may bring rewards in the short term, but these are not sufficient to ensure a secure foothold on the first rungs of Jacob's Ladder.

Nations also mature and evolve through the stages of the sephirot, as they have a group soul. Once you accept this possibility you can begin to understand why certain countries behave habitually according to the nature of their elected leaders, who act as the mother or father of the nation. For example, in the 1960s the United States, a comparatively young country, behaved like a typical adolescent, throwing its weight about in south-east Asia and acting in a bemused and outraged way when its interference was resented. By the mid-1970s the withdrawal from Vietnam and the Watergate scandal had brought the nation to the realisation that its parents (i.e. its leaders) were not infallible. This rude awakening inevitably led to widespread cynicism (or pragmatism, according to your perspective) and a desire for self-preservation that marked the move into adulthood.

If a nation can rise above self-interest and instead become self-aware, it will have matured to the level of Tiferet and see its problems diminish. It will no longer be so sensitive to issues of its self-image.

Such analysis is a necessary over-simplification, but it does demonstrate that sefirotic principles operate both in the individual and in the collective psyche.

6

The Way of Kabbalah

The popular perception of Kabbalah is that it is either a convoluted and deliberately abstract philosophy, of interest only to learned rabbinical scholars, or that it is an exclusive touchy-feely New Age fad practised by celebrities in search of an instant spiritual fix. In truth, Kabbalah expounds a simple philosophy, similar in one respect to Buddhism, in that it makes no distinction between sacred and secular life. Initiates are encouraged to consider their every action as an act of devotion to God and to be mindful of every moment.

Traditionally, the study of the Torah was central to Kabbalistic practice, but because of the unsettled state of the world at the present time, the work has had to be intensified and the once secret teachings disseminated to as many potential initiates as possible. Now anyone, Jew or gentile, can be initiated, provided that they undertake the work in the right spirit and demonstrate integrity and commitment. The spiritual secrets encoded in the Old Testament can now be taught as allegorical fables, and once guarded mystical techniques can be bought over the counter in any bookstore.

Devotion, contemplation and action

However, one aspect of Kabbalah remains unchanged: the necessity to engage the intellectual, psychological and physical aspects of the self so as to bring about transformation at every level. For this reason, equal emphasis is placed upon the three cornerstones of Kabbalistic practice: devotion, contemplation and action.

Devotion

The principle of devotion is expressed in the Ten Commandments, each one of which corresponds to a sefirotic sphere and defines right conduct at the intellectual, emotional and physical levels. It requires both self-discipline and love, which can be expressed in prayer or by counting one's blessings so as to acknowledge the presence of the divine in every aspect of life.

Contemplation

Meditation is the foundation of Kabbalistic practice, as well as being a proven method for improving health and well-being. Its purpose is to reveal how the divine will manifests in the world and in the pattern of one's own life. Suitable subjects for meditation would be the nature of God, the mystical significance of the Hebrew alphabet (see pages 104–5), the relationship between Kabbalah and astrology, and the apparent coincidences that may have facilitated significant meetings in your life.

Unfortunately, meditation does not come naturally to most Westerners, as we have been conditioned to believe that inactivity is self-indulgent and unproductive and therefore a waste of our precious time and resources. In fact, the reverse is true. Meditation affords the receptive student an opportunity for insight and understanding that no amount of time spent in study alone can bring. During meditation your body is in a state of deep relaxation but your mind is in a state of heightened awareness, in which it is possible to project consciousness beyond the physical body and into other realities, including the symbolic landscape of the psyche.

In meditation you conserve energy and may in fact acquire more power as you learn to channel the life force from the Earth and the ether to where it is most needed. Furthermore, by becoming acutely aware of the otherwise unconscious workings of your body you can stimulate the chakras to improve your circulation, revitalise your body and dispel energy blockages, which might otherwise lead to illness. And there are many other physical and psychological benefits to be derived from meditation, which space prohibits me from listing here.

Eastern traditions talk of meditation in abstract terms, encouraging the student to 'abide at the centre of their being', which Westerners often find difficult to understand. Kabbalalah takes a more psychological approach, viewing contemplation as simply the exercising of conscious control over the spheres governing thought, feeling and action, which are known collectively as the feeling triad (formed by Nezah, Hod and Yesod).

To appreciate what this means in practice, sit still for as long as you can and observe how your body protests against the imposition of the will. After only a few minutes you will find yourself fidgeting and demanding food or drink or a visit to the bathroom. Be sensible about this. Do not make yourself uncomfortable just to prove how much you can suffer. The point of this exercise is to become aware that your body is capable of wilfulness and needs to be trained to obey the superior will of the mind. If the physical discomfort is only a strategy to force you to end the exercise, the need for the drink or the toilet will subside. Otherwise, give in to it and resume the exercise afterwards.

Action

But meditation alone is not sufficient, as is evident from the number of 'bliss junkies' addicted to the sense of detachment attained in meditation and negligent of their worldly responsibilities. The Kabbalist needs to be grounded in the physical world so that when they draw down the dew of heaven it effects real and lasting change on earth. Neither is it sufficient to think positive thoughts or make plans to improve your life and that of those around you if you do not bring them into being.

The real meaning of action in modern Kabbalah is doing something with conscious intent combining work and worship in a single act, such as the making of ritual objects. This can be, for example, the preparation of an altar, the sketching of the Tree of Life for future study (see pages 31–2) or the creation of a set of Kabbalah cards (see page 108).

Another form of sacred action is healing, giving guidance and offering comfort or companionship. This can be as simple as striking up a conversation with an elderly neighbour so that they feel someone cares, or contributing to a charity – preferably by giving your time.

Devekut

A central aim of practical Kabbalah is the attainment of Devekut, conscious awareness of the divine at all times and in all things. Such a state is difficult to attain when there are so many distractions, but if you start small you will find that it is easier than you think.

Begin each morning by recording your dreams and then asking the blessing of the divine on your actions this day. Make your morning shower or wash a ritual cleansing by adding a prayer or invocation to the angels, asking that they draw near, and guide and protect you throughout the day. Be thankful for your breakfast and mindful as you eat it, rather than rushing through it while thinking about what you have to do next or watching the clock. Turn off the news and enjoy the stillness rather than digesting violence, heated arguments and injustice with your food.

In the same way that you can improve your physical health by walking short distances instead of taking the car, or replacing your mid-morning chocolate bar with an apple, so you can improve your spiritual well-being by taking bite-sized pieces of spiritual nourishment, giving new meaning to the phrase 'soul food'.

If you have time first thing in the morning, you could practise a ten-minute meditation. If not, try working one into your mid-morning coffee break, lunch hour or bedtime routine. You have to be a spiritual opportunist, snatching a few critical moments when you can. Don't wait for a half-hour window of opportunity in which you can practise an elaborate ritual. The chances are that you won't get one, and even if you do, you are likely to have unreasonable expectations that will spoil the experience. Instead, keep it small, stay focused and be always alert to the divine at work in the world around you. This is as essential to Kabbalah as the time you devote to study or committing the sefirotic scheme to memory. The cumulative effects of many five-minute reflections on a specific idea or aspect of Kabbalah can have a profound impact on your understanding and spiritual well-being.

Acknowledging the divine

Although Kabbalah emphasises the importance of ritual, contemplation and study, one of the most important aspects of the work is the spontaneous acknowledgment of the divine. If you feel thankful for all the blessings you have received or for a specific gift such as the birth of a child, the offer of a new job, the resolution of a problem, or healing, it is important to acknowledge this when the spirit takes you and not to wait for the time you designate for prayer or meditation. Such magical moments are the peak experience of spiritual practice, affording you a 'shortcut' up the Tree to connect with the source, albeit fleetingly.

Although advancement is in proportion to the amount of effort you apply to the work, tradition acknowledges the part providence can play in accelerating your progress. But providence only intervenes if you are ready to take advantage of the opportunities it affords and to acknowledge its existence. So do not feel self-conscious about surrendering to the unseen. Seize the moment. Let the angels, your guides and your own Higher Self know that you do not take them for granted and they will respond when you need them the next time.

Awakening to the divine

Some people see life as a burden to be endured until death brings release and the promise of lasting peace. For those who are terminally ill or suffering mental, physical or emotional abuse such an outlook is understandable. But even those of us who are blessed with a comparatively good life still indulge in moments of self-pity, resentment and regret, which diminishes our enjoyment and experience of the blessing that is life. We see every challenge as a problem dropped at random by fate to frustrate us and have been conditioned to expect life to play out like a soap opera in which bad news is always waiting in the wings. According to Kabbalah, life is not to be endured but to be enjoyed. We are not sinners born to suffer. We are divine sparks who have chosen to incarnate in order to experience life in a world we have created, and if we do not approve of the world then it is our responsibility to do what we can to improve it. Kick the debilitating habit of viewing life as a trial and see the world through new eyes.

We take even our closest friends and family for granted until they leave us. Practising Devekut means not waiting for that day to tell them how much you love them and what they mean to you.

If you have children, imagine that the next time you see them is the first time you have ever seen them in your life. Recall the time when you decided to have children and try to remember how eagerly you anticipated their birth (or adoption). Imagine how you would feel if you could have seen them as they are today without having to wait until they grew up. If you have been with them every day since their birth it is difficult to appreciate how far you have come together. Seeing with the eyes of the divine means being able to see the divine in all things. I defy any parent to look into their children's eyes and not see God.

You may be experiencing the conflict and frustration of dealing with an awkward teenager, but imagine that you are both much older and that you haven't seen each other for a long time. Perhaps they moved away or you drifted apart. You would bitterly regret those lost years and do anything to get them back. Any difficulties that you once had would seem trivial in the light of those precious years that are gone. If you were given a second chance, how would you recapture the closeness you once had? In reality, of course, you haven't lost that time, but you risk doing so if you cannot empathise with your son or daughter's difficulties and assist them rather than confronting them. Who cares whose fault it is? It takes two to make conflict and no-one can be completely blameless. Make it right before it is too late. See the situation with the eyes of God. See the divine in all things, because that is the way things are. This is not a New Age platitude devised to make you feel good. It's a fact. You are God and they are God, so put aside your pride and instead manifest unconditional love, which is the highest of the divine attributes that you possess.

Don't try to persuade them that you are right and that they are wrong, or that you know best because of your age and experience. Awaken their love for you by your example and your compassion, not by the weight of your argument or by demonstrating that your will is greater than theirs.

If you do not have children, instead see the divine in a beloved pet, your garden, your home, even your work. In fact, it is important that you should see the divine in your work, regardless of how difficult it might be. You are the only one who suffers if you are frustrated in your work, not your boss, your colleagues, your family or your partner. They only suffer your bad moods, and if you impose these upon them for too long they will eventually leave you to suffer your moods alone. If you cannot change your circumstances, then at least see the best in them until the situation improves. Even the worst job has the blessing of the divine upon it. Your task is to see it and to accept that it is better to be the caretaker whistling as he empties the dustbins than the managing director cursing his colleagues and heading for a coronary. Easier said than done? Not if you practise Devekut with sincerity.

Being honest with yourself

While it is comparatively easy to become consciously aware of the workings of the ego by observing your thoughts, feelings and actions at any particular moment, it takes a great deal of self-awareness to identify what triggers its responses. For example, you may feel uncomfortable accepting gifts or praise. On further examination, you may come to realise that this indicates a lack of self-worth, the inability to express emotion or a fear of rejection.

The reason why Kabbalah emphasises the importance of stability and integrity is that these qualities are the key that opens the path between the spheres of Yesod and Tiferet, facilitating access to the Higher Self. It is not that we are cut off from this all-knowing aspect of ourselves, but rather that we are usually oblivious to the still small voice within because the constant chatter of the ego invariably drowns it out.

To practise Kabbalah you need to be scrupulously honest with yourself and rise above the twin vices of wilfulness and lack of willpower to a state of willingness to serve the Higher Self. It is said that the ideal attitude for an initiate is to be as open and trusting as a child who knows that its parent has its best interests at heart.

Supplemental work: ten-minute meditation

Establish a daily ten-minute meditation routine. For the first week it is sufficient to sit in silence and empty your mind. Allow thoughts to arise, but do not attach any significance to them. Let go and simply be at peace with yourself.

In the second week try a simple visualisation. Imagine a small white dot in the distance. When you can hold that image for a few moments, draw it to you until it is the size of a door, then step through it. What do you find on the other side?

Healing

Healing is not something that is normally associated with Kabbalah, although there is a tradition of spiritual healing in Kabbalah known as Tikkun (meaning 'restoration'), which is perhaps the highest expression of Kabbalistic principles in action.

The difference between Kabbalistic healing and that practised by spiritualists and faith healers is that the Kabbalist is conscious of the specific process they have initiated whereas the spiritual healer works intuitively and talks more vaguely of channelling energy from the ether. The end result may be the same and the distinction may appear academic, but the Kabbalist has a clear idea of the context in which they work and the forces they are invoking. But this does not imply that the Kabbalist is superior to the intuitively gifted healer.

After appealing to the divine for permission to proceed, the Kabbalist will begin by laying their hands on the shoulders of the patient to establish physical contact in the world of Assiyah. Then they will raise their awareness to the psychological level of Yezirah, using their imagination to visualise the patient in full health, or a specific part of their anatomy restored to perfection where there is presently discomfort, a disorder or disease. Then, by drawing upon their compassion and empathy for the patient and consciously surrendering to the divine will, they soften their heart centre, which raises their awareness to the Tiferet of Beriah. At this point the crown of the psychological tree connects with the foundation of the world of spirit and they are able to appeal to the Elohim for divine intervention. Elohim is the name for the many forms in which God manifests at this level and translates as 'I will be manifest in many'. If grace is granted, new healthy cells will be generated in Beriah, which will then filter down to the matrix of etheric energy formed through the visualisation in Yezirah and be transferred through the healer to manifest in the patient. In this way new healthy tissue is called forth, created, formed and made as is everything else in manifest existence.

If the patient can accept that what they might consider to be a miracle has taken place, the etheric graft should take, but if they allow their disease to return, physical symptoms are likely to recur.

Supplemental work: giving healing

You can practise Kabbalah in action by giving healing on a regular basis. Healing is a natural phenomenon and in Kabbalah is considered a mizvah (a blessing) or act of devotion. But remember, you must never make any claims or promises and you are forbidden from making a diagnosis. It is permissible to tell the person receiving if you feel a cold spot, which indicates a blockage preventing energy from reaching a certain part of their body, but you must always refer them to a qualified medical practitioner if they complain of a chronic condition. You are offering a form of complementary therapy, not medical assistance.

You should not charge a fee, but you can instead accept a small donation for your chosen charity if it is offered.

It is not necessary to have the patient present. You can send healing by visualising the person sitting before you. This is called absent healing and may be necessary if the patient is in hospital or lives too far away for you to visit.

❖ Before the healing session, ground and centre yourself, otherwise you risk channeling your own life force into the patient, which will leave you drained and defeat the object of the exercise. When done correctly, healing benefits both the healer and the receiver.

❖ Before you start to work, ask your subject if they have had healing before and then explain what you are going to do. State clearly that you are not the source of the healing energy, but merely the channel. Tell them that there will be no further physical contact after you have made an empathic connection by putting your hands on their shoulders, as you will be working through the aura. Some people do not like to be touched by strangers (and may be too shy to say so), so this knowledge will reassure them. Healers, too, may feel self-conscious about physical contact, which will block the flow of energy. The more you can put the subject at their ease, the more receptive they will be and the more effective will be the healing.

❖ Next, ask the person receiving healing to remove their spectacles (if they have any) and to be seated and close their eyes.

❖ Now relax. You have nothing to prove. Your compassion for your patient will be sufficient to soften your heart centre at Tiferet and make you receptive to the healing energy flowing in through Keter, which you can visualise as light entering the crown of your head.

❖ Stand behind the subject and place your hands on their shoulders. Once you feel that you have a connection, scan their body from crown to toe using the palms of your hands. Hold your palms as close to their body as you can without touching – you are conducting the energy in through their aura, not their skin.

❖ You may feel a warmth in your hands or a tingling sensation, which the patient may remark upon. You may feel the need to close your eyes periodically, and if you do, you may see a colour in your mind's eye.

This is likely to be significant, as it can indicate the quality of energy that person needs or the area where the source of their problem lies, in which case concentrate on that area and visualise that colour emanating from your hands to dissolve the blockage or massage the pain at that point.

✤ Make it clear to the client when the treatment has finished, so they know they can open their eyes, and suggest that they sit still for a few moments, as it is not unusual for people to feel a little light-headed after healing.

✤ While they are doing so, wash your hands in cold water, otherwise you risk absorbing the essence of their disorder.

Supplemental work: creating a sacred space

If you can dedicate a spare room or even the corner of a room to ritual work, healing and prayer, you will find it very beneficial for focusing your mind. You can even use a cupboard if you are tight for space, or the top of a wooden chest, in which you can store the ritual objects (see page 74). This place will also serve as a private sanctuary to retire to when you need peace or when you are feeling low and need to raise your energy level, as it will become a vessel for the energy you generate during prayer and healing.

Your ritual space should contain two candlesticks to represent the outward pillars, an altar cloth (which should not be used for any other purpose) and a selection of items symbolising the four elements. When you stand before the candles you will represent the Pillar of Equilibrium as well as Consciousness and Will. The ritual items serve to focus your will on the objective and to contain the energy that will be released. You do not make an offering in Kabbalistic ritual, as there is no object of worship. However, a sacred statuette of an angel or an inspiring picture is allowed. If you are praying for healing or sending healing to someone, it can be helpful to have a photograph of that person before you.

The importance of ritual

When you are performing a ritual, be it a simple prayer of devotion, a healing, a request for guidance or an advanced magical ceremony, you need to work at all levels of awareness (spiritual, intellectual, emotional and physical) if the ritual is to be effective.

Whether you create a dedicated sanctuary for your rituals or simply sit in silence, your preparations should include a ritual wash. For simple rituals, your face and hands should be immersed in cold water. For more advanced rituals, it is customary to bathe and change into clothes that are worn exclusively on such occasions.

When you are ready, scan your body for tension to ensure that you are fully relaxed, then perform the Four Elements exercise (see pages 36–7) to ensure that you are fully body-conscious. Alternatively, perform the Tuning Up exercise (see pages 40–1) to establish the fact that all Kabbalistic practice begins and ends at Malkhut. This ensures that you will be able to integrate the energies you connect with and the insights you obtain into your waking consciousness, otherwise you risk reducing the experience to a mere spiritual sightseeing trip.

Grounding is also essential to ensure that you are not overwhelmed by any infusion of psychic energy, which could unbalance you, physically and psychologically. In all spiritual work you need to be receptive but rooted in reality, so that excess energy can be discharged into the ground as if you were a lightning conductor. If you doubt that such precautions are necessary, you have only to look at the example of the many eccentric occultists and notorious magicians such as Aleistair Crowley to see evidence of the psychological damage caused by too much knowledge and too little self-discipline.

Now you are ready to invoke the assistance of the Higher Self. Say a prayer or invocation in words of your own choosing. Ask for the blessing of the divine on your endeavour. Then visualise awakening the sefirot within the body in order of ascent from root to crown. Envisage them as unfolding lotus flowers, each in its appropriate colour, or as glowing spheres of divine energy. Finally, bring this awakening to its manifestation by lighting the candles, a symbol of the divine light manifesting from the darkness, while intoning 'Thy will be done' in acknowledgement of the Higher Will within and without.

When the ritual is complete, return to waking consciousness by envisaging the spheres closing one by one, in reverse, from Keter to Malkhut. Give thanks for the experience, insights or assistance received and stamp your feet to affirm contact with the physical world.

Supplemental work: philosophy

Having now grasped the basics of anatomy and the natural world, it is time to probe beyond the physical universe and familiarise yourself with the world of ideas. Choose a basic philosophy primer such as *Philosophy: 100 Essential Thinkers,* by Philip Stokes (Arcturus Publishing 2004), and read one section a week. You may find some of the answers you have been seeking, or you may identify a common thread on which to hang your own thoughts, or a means to test the validity of your own theories on the meaning of life.

Supplemental work: the world of the spirit

The final subject for study is, inevitably, the world of spirit. Go to your local library or book store and choose an anthology of the world's wisdom teachings from the wealth currently available and see how closely their insights reflect the teachings of Kabbalah. Over the course of the next few months, familiarise yourself with the principles of Buddhism, Taoism, Neoplatonism and so on, so that you can begin to appreciate how each culture and age expresses its yearning for reunion with the divine. This will help you to see your own beliefs in the context of a universal spiritual tradition, and you may also find inspiration, insights and subjects for reflection and meditation. Such books are food for the soul, which is just as much in need of nourishment as the body – even more so in times such as those we live in now.

Asking for divine intervention

Although the main purpose of practical Kabbalah is the acquisition of self-knowledge, there may come a time when you are presented with the opportunity to help others by acting as an intermediary between the worlds either by offering healing (see pages 71–3) or by bringing about a change in someone's personal circumstances. At such times you will need to have the interests of these individuals foremost in your mind and be acutely aware of your motivations for intervening. You must be scrupulously honest in your appraisal of the situation, as intervening in the lives of other people can have serious consequences both for their development and for your karma. If you suspect that you may have an ulterior motive, such as wishing to impress them with your powers or acquiring something at another person's expense, then you will be corrupting the knowledge you have obtained and your progress will be arrested, maybe even reversed. The key to acting correctly as an intermediary is intercession for the highest good of all concerned, not interference.

As someone capable of centring their consciousness in the Tiferet of the psyche so as to be aware of the three lower worlds simultaneously, you are in a unique position to see the consequences of your actions. In practice, this means trusting your intuition to tell you if and when it is right to act and whether or not the impulse comes from the Higher Self or the ego. This is not to say that the Kabbalist is more likely to have his prayers answered, as every appeal that comes from the heart is likely to be heeded, but simply to say that the Kabbalist is in a better position to know when to intercede on someone else's behalf, how to ask and what to ask for.

As an example, I once found myself invited to stay overnight with a married couple. I had only just met the husband but felt a strong affinity with him and a strong suspicion that our meeting was engineered for a specific purpose. That evening the couple's difficulties came to a head and they decided to separate. I had no desire nor right to interfere in their relationship, but I felt that my friend was suffering needlessly. I centred myself at Tiferet, to view the situation from the perspective of the Higher Self, and asked for his suffering to be alleviated and for divine intervention so that these two people's needlessly destructive relationship might be resolved according to the divine will.

It was important that I did not specify a particular outcome or determine how the matter should be resolved, but only asked that my friend should not suffer any longer and that both partners should find their true path and their true place in the world. Within a few months they had divorced amicably, and soon afterwards my friend remarried and had the child he had always hoped for with a woman who was clearly his soul mate in every sense of the word.

7

Dreamwork

Many of our aspirations, anxieties and fantasies are unconscious, and as such they can adversely affect our view of reality. However, there are techniques for identifying and addressing these issues. The most common and easily accessible method is the study and interpretation of dreams.

Most of our dreams are inconsequential and involve the processing of data and impressions gleaned from the day. It is comparatively simple to recognise the circumstances that have been scrambled into a dream scenario and to identify the characters as composites of people seen the previous day. But as we drift into the deeper stages of sleep we are able to access other states of awareness corresponding to higher triads on the Tree. It is these that require serious study. Those that relate to our personal development are experienced at the soul level, above the functional triad of personal ego consciousness, while prophetic dreams are experienced at the level of the spirit. The fourth level involves direct contact with the divine, but these states of awareness are extremely rare.

Dreams concerned with personal development are relatively easy to identify. They are vivid and tend to remain in the mind long after the imagery has faded. They are usually indicative of a crisis, a decision that needs to be made or an issue that needs to be resolved. And although the imagery may seem obscure, it tends to consist of universal symbols, the meaning of which can be found in any reliable reference book on the subject. The inhabitants of such dreams are invariably aspects of the dreamer's own personality, each with their own perspective on the problem, and appear in order to assist in the resolution of the issue.

Sometimes such dreams offer a clear confirmation that we have made the right decision. For example, during the course of writing this book I decided to take a break and consult a valued source to confirm that what I had written was in accordance with tradition. That night I dreamt that I was embarking on a journey with my family, but I soon became separated from them in the crowds at the railway station. Knowing intuitively that they would be all right, I decided to continue the journey alone, but I found myself on the wrong train. I didn't feel anxious, as I knew I could change at the next station and catch another back to the terminal. As I made my way to the return train, a ticket inspector appeared and reassured me that it was easy to become confused at such a busy station.

The railway station was an obvious symbol for the inner journey to self-discovery, which we must take alone, and the main station was the junction I had reached at this stage of my understanding. Taking the wrong train indicated that I had run ahead of myself, so to speak, and needed to retrace my steps and make sure of basic principles before I ventured out again. All this is self-evident, but what is interesting is the appearance of the ticket inspector, who symbolises the Higher Self, or inner teacher. Although he was a separate character in the dream, I remember relating to him as if I was speaking through him and listening to him as the lost traveller at the same time. Such distinctions should become clear as you study your own dreams.

Prophetic dreams are more unusual, but there are numerous recorded cases confirming that such insights are possible (see the following section).

Kabbalah places great emphasis on the art of dream interpretation, which has been a specialised study of initiates for thousands of years and which is endorsed by several key myths in the Torah. The story of Joseph is a good example. The significance of Joseph's imprisonment in Egypt is only fully understood when it is known that the Hebrew word for Egypt means 'confined' and that Joseph's multi-coloured coat is symbolic of the soul.

The story can then be interpreted as an allegorical journey into incarnation, with dreams serving as fleeting glimpses into the nature of existence.

Precognitive dreams – a dream of death

Precognitive dreams are rare, but when they occur they invariably foreshadow a significant event. Internationally renowned psychic artist Sylvia Gainsford, illustrator of my own Kabbalah cards, experienced a precognitive dream of her own death. She says:

> During my teens I was a boarder at a teaching training college in Brighton and was in the habit of swapping dreams every morning with my room-mate. One morning I told her about the previous night's dream, in which our class went on an outing into the town. In the dream we were walking on a rough track through the rain, prompting someone to say to a friend of ours, 'It's a good job you've got your mac on, Mike.' Then a friend of ours, Martin, asked what my friend and I were going to have for our meal that evening. We jokingly replied 'Mrs B's eternal soup', which was the name we gave our landlady's soup. At which point a black car suddenly appeared round the corner, mounted the pavement and knocked me down. The dream ended with Martin, who had a connection with the church, standing over me making the sign of the cross and dipping his finger in Mrs B's eternal soup as if it was holy water. It was a surreal ending but very vivid and detailed.

> Later that day we went on an outing with the class. It was raining and we found ourselves on the same rough track that I had dreamt about. Someone said, 'It's a good job you've got your mac on, Mike', just as they had in the dream, and then Martin asked us what we were having for our meal that evening. Before I could reply, my friend pulled me back and a moment later a black car came careering out of control round the corner and mounted the pavement. I'm certain I would have been killed had I not told my friend that dream. Fortunately, I had described everything in detail to her that morning, so I have proof that I dreamt it, but I still can't explain how such foresight is possible.

Exercise: improving dream recall

Do this exercise each night before you go to sleep.

❖ Close your eyes and review the events of the day in your mind. If you recall anything unpleasant, view it with detachment and let it pass out of your mind. This process will clear insignificant impressions so that you can access the unconscious without being distracted by irrelevant images. It will also reduce the risk of nightmares because it will give you the opportunity to identify and address anything that might be troubling you.

❖ Next, visualise yourself lying in bed enjoying a peaceful sleep. See the hands on your bedside clock moving through the hours as if captured by time lapse photography. Through the curtains you glimpse clouds drifting across the face of the moon and the stars shining brightly in the night sky. Now see the sun come up and its warming radiance filling your room with light.

❖ Visualise yourself waking up and recording the details of your dreams in your bedside journal (see page 81).

❖ Say to yourself three times, 'I will remember my dreams.' This should ensure both a restful sleep and improved dream recall.

Exercise: dialogue with your dreams

One of the most effective methods of establishing contact with the unconscious, Higher Self or inner guide is to enter into a dialogue with the characters in your dreams immediately upon waking. But to do so you have to be honest with yourself and let the 'conversation' flow without thinking too much about what you're saying until you are ready to analyse the imagery later on.

Carl Jung, the founder of analytical psychology, who disagreed with Freud's assertion that all neurosis is sexual in origin, considered such techniques essential for achieving psychic wholeness. According to Jung:

> To the degree that [a person] does not admit the validity of the other person [in the dream] he denies 'the other' within himself the right to exist – and vice versa. The capacity for inner dialogue is a touchstone for outer objectivity.

❖ Close your eyes and when you are suitably relaxed visualise yourself returning to the scene of your dream.

❖ Take the part of each of the people in your dream one at a time and speak as you feel they might have done if the dream had continued from this point on. Express their mood in your own words and say what you imagine they came to say. You may find that each articulates an aspect of your own personality (see Who's Who in Your Dreams, page 86). It is not necessary to interpret the meaning of the dream. What is important is to use the dream to understand how you feel about the situation you dreamt, what your attitude is to the characters and what message they may have for you.

Exercise: keeping a dream journal

Although only a small proportion of your dreams may be significant, you will be able to identify them only if you a keep a dream journal so that you can make an accurate record of the imagery and symbols for later analysis. As you become familiar with the significance of dream symbolism you will begin to make connections of your own and come to your own conclusions without having to refer to reference books. This will strengthen your connection with the unconscious and heighten your psychic sensitivity, and you will begin to experience increasingly meaningful dreams.

❖ If you think that you might have dreamt of something that later actually happened, you will be able to go back and check the details of your dream to confirm that it was precognitive.

❖ If you have a lucid dream (one in which you realise that you are dreaming and then take control of the dream), note the scene and the sensations the moment you awake, otherwise your rational mind will try to explain the dream away as the product of your imagination.

❖ If you are fortunate enough to experience a so-called 'great dream', one of spiritual insight, note every detail on waking, as the symbolism will be highly significant (see pages 83–6).

Buy a diary with a day to a page and put it by your bed, together with a ballpoint or felt tip pen. When you wake, immediately make a note of the key events and images. This will help you to recall more information before it recedes into the unconscious. If you write the last episode in great detail, you risk losing the fleeting impressions of earlier dreams. You can sketch in the details later, using the highlights to jog your memory.

Exercise: triggering a lucid dream

Just before drifting off to sleep, affirm in words of your own choosing that you are going to experience a deep restful, revitalising sleep and that you are going to become conscious of the fact that you are dreaming when you see a certain symbol. This could be a door that you will want to enter, a garden you would like to explore, or an animal or a person that you expect to meet in the dream. Whatever symbol you choose, it should be something with positive associations. Affirm that when you see this symbol you will take control of the dream and explore it at will.

It is unlikely that you will be successful on your first attempt at this exercise, so be patient.

Supplemental work: dream themes

To evaluate your progress so far, take 20 minutes at the end of your first week of dream recording to read through the entries in your dream journal. Ask yourself:

❖ What were the main themes of this week's dreams?

❖ What have my dreams revealed about my physical, emotional, mental and spiritual states?

❖ Has my dream recall noticeably improved?

❖ How many dreams did I recall at the end of the week compared with the first two nights? (If you can recall more than two dreams a night in detail, you are making considerable progress. If not, be patient. Your powers of recall will improve within a few weeks.)

❖ What have I learnt about myself from analysing my dreams?

❖ Am I beginning to distinguish between dreams of no consequence and those with psychological and psychic significance?

❖ Can I identify those dreams that relate to the physical, emotional, psychological and spiritual levels of awareness?

Look at the diary again and underline any significant symbols and characters (you can use the Dream Dictionary on pages 83–6 to help you). Ask yourself:

❖ Can I eliminate any imagery that was directly influenced by what I saw on TV or experienced personally that week?

❖ From what remains, can I identify any recurring themes?

❖ Do certain symbols seem more significant in the light of subsequent dreams?

❖ Am I starting to be able to use my increasing knowledge and intuition to analyse symbols that are not listed in the dream dictionary?

If your dream recall is continuing to improve and you have established the habit of keeping a dream diary, you can move on to probe the unconscious through meditation and visualisation.

The dream dictionary

Use this key to the most significant symbols, situations and themes to interpret your dreams.

Activities

CLIMBING, WALKING: Ambition. A never-ending climb suggests striving for something unattainable. Ladders usually represent professional or social ambitions; mountain paths are symbolic of a spiritual search for meaning in life; while stairs correspond to our attitude to life, narrow, steep stairs suggesting that we expect difficulties, stairs to the basement representing a willingness to face our fears or suppressed memories.

DEATH: change.

DIGGING, SEARCHING: the need to probe the unconscious to recover repressed memories, or the search for the true self.

EATING: a hunger for affection.

FLYING AND FALLING: an internalisation of an out-of-body experience.

PACKING, TIDYING, CLEARING OUT: readiness for change.

RUNNING: running after something or somebody suggests a fear of loss; being chased indicates an unwillingness to face fears or facts.

SITTING AN EXAM: fear of having your beliefs tested.

SWIMMING: being carried along by a fast-moving current indicates helplessness; swimming in calm, warm water symbolises love and security.

UNDRESSING IN PUBLIC: feelings of restriction, inhibition, inadequacy or insecurity.

Significant objects

BOOKS: memories.

BROKEN OBJECTS: fear that we are not fulfilling our potential.

KEYS: a solution to something that has troubled us. If the answer is not revealed in the dream itself, re-enter the dream in your imagination as soon as you wake up and follow it through to its conclusion, or meditate on it, using clues recorded in your dream journal.

MONEY: self-worth. Being robbed or losing money suggests that we feel our efforts are being undermined by others.

PHOTOGRAPHS AND PAINTINGS: often self-portraits, revealing either your true nature or how you perceive yourself at this moment in your life. They can even offer a glimpse of the person you were in a past life.

TOYS: a desire to return to the innocence of childhood, or the desire to confide our feelings to someone we can trust.

Significant situations

BEING TRAPPED: a fear of being restricted or overwhelmed by responsibilities and commitments.

FIGHT, VIOLENT ARGUMENT: inner conflict, or the need to express anger in waking life.

PARALYSIS, HELPLESSNESS: indecision and lack of confidence.

PARTIES: well-being and contentment. If you are the host and no-one has turned up, this indicates a fear of being a social outcast or that you feel disappointed in others.

TRAVEL: one of the most significant recurring themes, indicative of our progress through life and our expectations of what lies ahead.

WEDDINGS: can be purely a wish-fulfilment fantasy, but usually suggests that the dreamer is testing their attitude towards commitment and responsibility in general.

Significant places

AIRPORTS, RAILWAY STATIONS, COACH TERMINALS: suggest that we have come to a point in life where we need to consider who we are, what we really want from life and where we need to go to get it.

BANKS: frequently symbols of authority.

CASTLES: a wary, defensive and insular personality.

DOORS: opportunities. Those that readily open reveal a willingness to try new experiences and indicate that the dreamer expects little resistance to their plans and ambitions, whereas doors that are heavy or difficult to open indicate a lack of confidence or anticipated difficulties.

GARDENS: can reveal a lot about our temperament. An overgrown jungle indicates an unwillingness to face problems and a reluctance to deal with unresolved issues, while a neat, formal garden could suggest a conservative nature and a need for order and stability in life. A rambling cottage garden or a meadow of wild flowers symbolises a relaxed, easy-going attitude and a willingness to live in the present moment. The colour of the flowers can also be significant, with vibrant hues symbolising physical energy, strong emotions and enthusiasm for life, and pastel shades indicating preoccupation with the intellect and spiritual matters.

GATES: traditionally represent a partner, heavy, stiff gates indicating someone who is resistant to change and small gates a person who is too compliant.

HOSPITALS: fear of being controlled by or at the mercy of others, especially those with superior knowledge or power.

HOUSES: our home, furnishings and possessions express our personality and attitude to the outside world, while the house itself represents our current state of mind. If the house is old-fashioned, it can be an expression of a conservative nature and concern with one's security and personal comfort. If it is modern, you are more likely to be open to new ideas. If the exterior is in contrast with the interior, this may indicate concern with keeping up a facade to impress other people.

LIBRARIES: a storehouse of memories and self-knowledge.

ROOMS: dark, cluttered rooms indicate a reluctance to let go of the past, while light, spacious rooms symbolise openness to new ideas and opportunities, and a willingness to live in the moment.

Attics: hidden memories.

Bathroom and toilet: concerns about our health.

Bedrooms: a need for privacy and personal space.

Cellars: our deepest fears.

Kitchens and dining rooms: our attitude to food, which is in turn symbolic of emotional and spiritual nourishment and also our appetite for life.

Living rooms: the décor and condition of the living room can reveal our attitude to family, friends and society.

SCHOOLS, COLLEGES, UNIVERSITIES: a setting in which we try to resolve a conflict between what was expected of us in our youth and our achievements to date.

SHOPS: a setting in which we are forced to make a significant choice.

WALLS AND FENCES: high boundaries suggest a defensive, distrustful personality, low ones an openness.

WINDOWS: through the windows we perceive the outside world. A rugged landscape with overcast skies suggests a pessimistic nature and an unwillingness to see obstacles as problems to be overcome.

Who's who in your dreams

It is a commonly held belief among those who make a serious study of dreams that each character represents an aspect of the dreamer's personality, with the obvious exception of people we know in waking life.

✤ A child can symbolise the innocent, unworldy aspect of ourselves and might appear in scenes involving a search for security or the uncovering of significant events in our past.

✤ A youth expresses our energy and ambitions.

✤ An adult often symbolises increasing maturity and appears when there are issues of responsibility and commitment to be resolved.

✤ An older person can represent significant changes, particularly those to do with letting go of the past.

<u>8</u>

Practical Steps to Self-empowerment

Psychological Kabbalah is not simply concerned with issues of self-awareness and recognising personal strengths and weaknesses. It also offers practical solutions and techniques so that you can reach your full potential. In this chapter, we are going to look at some of those techniques.

Goal setting

Before you can begin this process you need to ask yourself two questions: 'What do I really want?' and 'What do I really need?' – while recognising that the two are not necessarily the same. Some people want to be famous, but they actually fear success because of the responsibilities it brings and the possibility that they may lose control of their lives, so they undermine their efforts with self-destructive strategies to ensure that they always fail – and always have an excuse. In this way, many talented people have fallen by the wayside bemoaning the fickleness of fate, while less gifted individuals have lived their dream because they were tenacious and determined. Your ambitions may be more modest and conventional, but you still need to look at the reality behind your desires.

Next you need to ask yourself what qualities are required to attain your goal and what steps you need to take in order to arrive there. Although success may appear to scoop some fortunate individuals up and carry them from obscurity to a better or more 'privileged' life, few actually achieve anything without having prepared themselves in some way so as to be ready when opportunity knocks. Everything worth having has to be earned. If you get lucky, it is for a reason, and there will be a price to pay. That is not to say that good fortune is not possible or that fate will spoil your fun, only that with every step on the ladder your integrity is tested.

Exercise: your future self

Once you have a goal in mind and have identified what qualifications and experience you will need to achieve it, it can be useful to visualise a typical day in your desired life to see if you really want it – otherwise you may find it was the unobtainable aspect of the thing you craved rather than the thing itself.

Relax, close your eyes and imagine a typical day when you have all that you are now working for. See yourself waking in the morning and going through your daily routine. Then do it again and again. You may discover that the novelty of your ideal lifestyle wears thin after a while. Or that there are unseen aspects that are not so appealing. Perhaps you want to be a writer because you are frustrated in your present employment, but maybe you haven't considered how isolated you might feel or how much self-discipline is needed to sit down at the computer from 9am to 5pm every day and to be prepared to go back to it in the evening and work all weekend to meet a deadline.

Or maybe you want to start your own business because you hate working for someone else. Visualising your day might make you realise that you will have to work even harder for yourself than you do for your present employer.

If you are still eager to realise your dream and feel that it is right for you, then the visualisation has confirmed your future path and you can pursue it with confidence.

Exercise: identifying your life's purpose

We all wonder from time to time what our purpose in life might be, particularly if things are not going according to our plans. We need to know that we are on the right path and not merely passing the time or, worse, pursuing a lost cause. Well, fortunately there is a simple, direct method for connecting with that eternal aspect of yourself that knows why you chose to incarnate.

✤ Sit quietly and visualise yourself standing before a full length mirror. How would you describe your physical appearance? Be honest. Remain detached. This is only your temporary physical form. It is functional, like a car that you require to take you from A to B. It does not need to be aesthetically pleasing, only reliable and well maintained.

✤ Now see a reflection of a scene from earlier in the day when you interacted with other people. How would you describe your emotions?

Are you even-tempered or quick to anger? Are you anxious or excitable? Are you easily upset or do you mask your emotions?

❖ Now recall a recent episode when you were engaged in thought or a discussion. How would you describe your intellectual capacity? Are you philosophical or pragmatic? Do you have a gift for language, ideas, numbers or organisation? What are your talents? How would you evaluate your understanding of certain subjects at school, in further education and at work? Have you ever studied a subject for its own sake, even though there was no qualification at the end of it? Is there a topic you have always wanted to learn about but haven't been given the opportunity to study? Do not be critical. Accept that this summary is who you were and not necessarily who you are now.

Now you are going to access another level of your being, one of which you are not consciously aware. It is your spirit, and its aspirations also need to be addressed.

❖ Visualise yourself sitting in the shade of a low-hanging tree in a beautiful garden. In fact, the garden is more than beautiful, as it is the garden of heaven. You are here in the company of several members of your soul group, with whom you are about to incarnate. It is many years ago, in the resting period between this life and the last. You are discussing who you will be and what you need to achieve. What do you wish for yourself? What commitment did you make to improve yourself and the world you are about to enter?

❖ When you are ready, return to waking consciousness in the usual way and take a few moments to reflect on the insights you have obtained. Affirm that you chose your body, your emotional make-up and your intellectual capacity for a particular purpose. Be comfortable and content with yourself as you are.

Moods

Most us tend to think of ourselves as being at the mercy of our moods. In contrast, Kabbalah teaches that we can control our moods but that we choose to relinquish that power because we get a buzz out of riding on the rollercoaster of our emotions. As long as our moods are not too extreme and we are able to rein them in when we really need to, we indulge them in order to feel more alive. We all know that the ideal is to achieve inner peace, but most people are not ready for tranquillity. We need a little anxiety and the unexpected in our lives if we are to avoid boredom. But with maturity comes the realisation that endless activity and entertainment is not the only way to feel alive. In fact, it merely passes the time rather than uses it. In contrast, sitting in stillness and serenity affords us the opportunity to appreciate what we have, to identify what we need as opposed to what we want, and to connect with our true self, which is our best friend, our own personal guru and our guardian angel.

When we consider it in these terms it is a wonder why we indulge our moods to the degree that we do. We have the answers to all our questions within, if only we would take the time to be still and listen. In such a state we would come to the realisation that our habitual mood swings only create instability and insecurity.

Observing your moods at different points in the day is another way of raising your awareness of the dynamics of the feeling triad and, most important, of taking control of them. If you can do this, you are less likely to be disturbed by other people's bad moods and more likely to stabilise your environment by your own example. If you are calm under pressure, those around you will unconsciously gravitate towards you in order to come under your influence, and the atmosphere will change from one of anxiety, agitation and tension to one of determination to deal with problems with detachment.

Remember, we all have free will, but few of us exercise it. Study the relationship between the spheres in the feeling triad and make them the subject of a meditation at least once a week. Exercise your will over the wilfulness of your body by committing yourself to a chosen task and seeing it through. Mastering your emotions does not mean suppressing them, but stabilising them under the authority of your will. Doing so will strengthen your character and demonstrate your reliability, which will earn you the respect of everyone you meet.

Supplemental work: observe your moods

For one week observe your moods at specific times of the day. Notice your mood at the end of the week. Note also how you react to other people – your family, friends, neighbours and colleagues. Note if their reactions, mood or behaviour affects your own. You may be surprised to discover that your moods are a habitual reaction, determined by the weather, the time of day and so on, rather than your true feelings and that it is therefore difficult for other people to affect your mood. Compare your notes to identify any patterns in your moods.

Becoming aware of your own inner state in this way is the first step towards self-awareness and will increase your sensitivity to the workings of the upper triads.

Supplemental work: write a letter

Set aside 15–20 minutes every day for a week to write a letter to someone you do not see or hear from very often but who you think might like to hear from you. It could be a parent, a relative, an old friend or even an ex-colleague or teacher who might care to hear how you are doing and how things have changed since they saw you last. Choose a time when you generally feel low or lethargic and force yourself to sit down and write. Impose your will on your sluggish lower self and be aware of how your mood alters as you write from one of self-centred teenage-like indolence (which is the influence of Yesod, the ego) to one of emotional altruism (which is the manifestation of Tiferet, the Higher Self).

The letter doesn't have to be more than a page or two, but it shouldn't be considered a chore to be dashed off and done with, rather a labour of love, written in your neatest handwriting and expressing a genuine interest in the recipient's well-being.

This simple task combines the three central disciplines of Kabbalah, contemplation, devotion and action, and it will be of practical benefit to two people: you and the person whose day will be that bit brighter because you have demonstrated how you value them by making the effort to write to them.

Resolving conflict

When we are engaged in any form of personal growth programme that involves intense self-analysis it is easy to forget that other people are equally complex personalities. We will often forgive ourselves for the occasional outburst of anger or inconsistency in our behaviour, but rarely are we as forgiving of others.

This lack of empathy is the root of many of our problems. We are conditioned from an early age to see other people as falling into one of two distinct categories, good and bad. As we grow, we learn that there are many shades of grey and that behaviour is largely determined by upbringing and circumstances. Too many of us allow ourselves to be manipulated by the populist media, who reinforce these childhood stereotypes because it makes for more dramatic programming.

There is little we can do to combat this 'dumbing down' of important issues other than to switch off and make an effort to be better informed. But when it comes to personal disagreements there are effective ways to avoid a conflict. One of the great Kabbalaists urged us to treat others as we would like to be treated and to love our neighbour, but such compassion is hard to attain and sustain. The following exercise provides the first crucial step to creating a connection with another person so that you can defuse a potential confrontation or see a dispute from their perspective and thereby resolve it for your mutual benefit.

Exercise: attaining equilibrium

❖ Sit in a chair and close your eyes. Focus on your breath.

❖ When you are fully relaxed, shift your attention to the right side of your face. Sense the facial muscles and the blood pumping through the veins on this side of your face and the heat in your skin. Become acutely aware of your right ear, the air circulating across the fine hairs and the sounds outside reaching your inner ear as subtle vibrations. Now shift your awareness to your right eye and the weight of the upper eyelid resting on the lower one. Be aware of the eyeball and the lubricating fluid that enables it to swivel in the socket. Shift to the muscles on the right side of your forehead and the almost imperceptible weight of your hair resting on your scalp.

❖ Once you have successfully focused your awareness on the right side of your face, leaving the other a blank, shift to the left side and repeat the process.

✤ Consider how you are able to shift your emotional focus as easily as you shift the focus of your attention from one side of your body to the other. The result is seemingly contradictory moods and conflicting signals, which you are probably not even conscious of sending to others. Can you appreciate the fact that they are able to do exactly the same and that as such they are neither 'obstinate', 'inconsiderate' nor any of the other adjectives you may have attributed to them? They are as complex and self-centred as you are. You are seeing only one aspect of their multi-faceted personality, just as they see only one side of you.

✤ Now focus your attention on a point in the middle of your forehead. Feel the energy pulsing in this crucial centre commonly known as the third eye. You can stimulate it by putting the tip of your index finger close to the skin and making small circles in a clockwise direction, but avoid contact with the skin. You may feel a tingling sensation or a dull pressure as the third eye opens and the energy is activated.

✤ When you have a sense of the energy in your third eye, visualise a line of this energy extending like a laser beam down to the centre of your chest. Sense the chakra here dissolving. The warmth of the energy from this chakra now runs like liquid down to a point beneath your navel and awakens the solar plexus chakra, which radiates a warmth across your abdomen and lower back.

✤ Feel that all tension has been dissolved. The feeling is so good that you want to share it with others, even those with whom you have a conflict. You know beyond a doubt that if they could feel this way, they would have no anger or antagonism towards you or anyone else.

✤ When you are ready, return to waking consciousness and stamp your feet to ground yourself. Once you have had time to assimilate this experience, consider how you might resolve your difficulty with the other person.

Bereavement and grief

We all deal with loss in different ways and experience grief to different degrees. While none of us can avoid the grieving process, which involves denial, anger, helplessness, pining and finally acceptance, we can minimise the degree to which we suffer by working through exercises such as the one below in order to adjust to a life without the presence of our loved one and accept the idea that they now exist in another reality. You may think that such solutions are particular to modern psychology, but the technique used in this exercise is based on a traditional Kabbalistic method known as The

Fixing. Even in earlier times, Kabbalah did not only offer the initiate a path to enlightenment but also served as a form of psychotherapy, or healing of the soul.

It is always important to prepare yourself prior to any form of spiritual work, but it is even more so when there is a possibility of self-deception or psychological disturbance due to the pain of loss. Your overwhelming desire to be reunited with a loved one can influence the experience and distort the impressions you receive. It is therefore imperative that you work through the Tuning Up visualisation on pages 40–1 and ask for the assistance of your inner guide before undertaking the following exercise.

Exercise: letting go

To strengthen your connection with the person you have lost, you may choose to play their favourite piece of music or place their favourite flowers nearby. Alternatively, you could hold a photograph or a personal object that belonged to them, or do something they liked in order to draw them near. Many mediums believe that the spirits of the departed continue to derive pleasure from whatever they enjoyed doing in life, so do not feel self-conscious if that means playing a musical instrument or reading aloud from their favourite book. It might even mean cooking their favourite meal – after all, such ritual offerings to one's ancestors are customary in many cultures even today. But do not attempt such things if they upset you. The aim of this exercise is to achieve closure, not to reopen emotional wounds. If you feel strong and centred, you could even go to a favourite place you shared, such as a park, and perform the exercise as a visualisation, but do not do so if you fear that you may be overwhelmed by your emotions. A bad experience will only intensify your unhappiness. Make this a happy reunion, or at least an experience that brings you peace of mind.

I want to make it absolutely clear at this point that this exercise is NOT concerned with summoning the spirits of the dead. It is merely a conversation with a loved one, who may or may not choose to respond. It is a chance to clear unresolved issues and say goodbye. And, as you will see, the most important aspect is that it gives you the chance to do something for the departed person, so that they too can achieve closure, let go of their earthly concerns and move on. But if you feel uncomfortable with the concept, leave it for another time.

Note: Do not attempt this exercise if you are experiencing trauma or suffering abnormal grief. If you are unable to accept the loss of a loved one, you may need to consult a qualified bereavement counsellor and work through the grieving process with them.

✤ Having made your intentions clear by creating a conducive atmosphere and preparing yourself with ritual ablutions and prayer, it is now time to cast a protective circle of white light around you. Even the most experienced mediums use a routine of grounding, prayer and protection before and after every session so that they can remain focused and minimise the chance of self-deception. Close your eyes and allow your thoughts to subside. When you have quietened your mind, visualise a small speck of white light in the centre of your forehead. Imagine it becoming larger, until it is about the size of a tennis ball, and sense its radiance intensifying. Now visualise it expanding until it encircles your head, then see it slowly sinking to the floor, encasing you in a circle of protective divine energy.

✤ When you are grounded and centred, invoke the Archangels for protection and to intensify the energy field around you. Do so using the following words:

> In the name of Adonai, the One God, I ask this blessing. If it is thy will may the presence of the Archangels fill this space with their light, compassion and healing energy. Before me, Raphael; behind me Gabriel, by my right hand Michael, by my left hand Uriel, and above me shines the Shekhinah, the living presence of God.

Now sense the Archangels approaching from the four corners, illuminating the room.

✤ In whatever words feel appropriate, ask that you may become aware of the presence of the person with whom you want to communicate. If it is a woman, you may smell their favourite scent, and if it is a man who smoked, you may smell their tobacco. You may even feel their touch stroking you gently on the cheek or patting your hair. If so, do not be alarmed. They merely want to reassure you that they consent to this connection.

✤ If you sense nothing at all, visualise a white light in the corner of the room. Watch as it grows in size and intensity. Now watch as the person emerges from the centre of the light to stand before you. If you are overcome with emotion, do not repress your feelings. Evidently, they need to be cleared. Do not be surprised if the person appears younger than when they died and in radiant health, as this is their true self.

✤ Now engage in a conversation with the deceased. Allow your thoughts to arise spontaneously and listen for their answer. They may not speak but instead might offer a gift or a symbol, whose significance should be self-evident.

✤ Finally, ask if you can do anything for them. Maybe they have unfinished business, or maybe they have something they wished to say to someone but passed away before they had the chance to. Perhaps they simply want to urge you to let them go and make the most of the rest of your life.

✤ When the conversation comes to a natural conclusion, the departed person's image will fade as they return to the light. Thank the Archangels for their protection and then close the circle by visualising it rising up to the level of your head and being reabsorbed into the third eye centre in the middle of your forehead. Ground yourself once again by stamping your feet, rinsing your hands in cold water or going for a walk in the fresh air.

Coping with other forms of loss

The death of a loved one is not the only form of loss. A divorce or separation from a partner, for example, can be just as difficult as a bereavement; redundancy can have a serious effect on some people, particularly if they have given many years of service to a single employer and their sense of identity has been defined by their work.

In such cases you can adapt the Letting Go exercise on pages 94–5 by replacing the figure in the light with your ex-partner, friends, colleagues, or yourself in perfect health. In this case the image is created by your imagination to enable you to connect with the other person(s) or other aspect of yourself on a psychic level, but the effect will be equally beneficial and the experience is as real. The other individual (if there is one) may not be aware of what you are doing but they will feel a vague sense of relief, as if a burden has been lifted from their shoulders. As a result, you should see a shift in their attitude towards you as the ties that bind you are broken. If the exercise concerns your relationship with an aspect of yourself, you should likewise experience a positive shift in your attitude.

2

Developing Psychic Powers

Contrary to popular belief, we are all born with psychic abilities, but few of us choose to develop them. Some confuse psychic ability with superhuman powers and dismiss the possibility that such phenomena exist outside of fantasy fiction. They consider themselves above such nonsense and go through life in a state of blissful ignorance of the greater reality around them. Others may have experienced such common phenomena as precognition (intuitively knowing that someone will phone or visit them before they do so), but they may be afraid that if they develop their gift they will be dabbling in the occult and opening themselves up to mischievous or evil influences.

Kabbalah teaches that psychic ability is merely an extension of our awareness beyond the limitations of the physical body and that it develops naturally as we become more self-aware and receptive to the life force generated by all living things. It can involve clairvoyance (for example, reading the aura, or human energy field), remote viewing (projecting your own consciousness to other locations), out-of-body experiences (projecting your consciousness into other dimensions), psychometry (picking up visual impressions from personal objects in which the owner has left a residue of their personal energy) or mediumship (becoming highly intuitive and sensitive to the feelings of others and to the presence of those no longer incarnate). In isolation, psychic ability may be merely a fascinating phenomenon, but in the context of personal development within the study of Kabbalah it can be a useful indication of your rate of progress. To develop such abilities you will need to begin to trust your intuition and to practise visualisations such as Feeling the Auric Field on pages 98–9 in order to stimulate the third eye, the organ of psychic sight.

Exercise: seeking guidance

If there is a decision you are finding it difficult to make or a situation you need to see beneath the surface of, try this exercise.

Think about the problem or situation for a few moments, then close your eyes and let the images arise. If you see nothing, visualise a small light in the distance, the size and brightness of a star, and allow yourself to be drawn towards it. An image or scene should appear, which will reveal the solution to the problem or the truth of the situation through your third eye. This image or scene symbolises how you perceive the situation in your unconscious mind and will be more revealing than what you can see with normal sensory perception.

Once you have stimulated the third eye in this way, you can use the following exercises over the course of the next few weeks and months to develop your sensitivity.

Exercise: feeling the auric field

❖ Place your hands about 30 centimetres (12 inches) apart, with the palms facing one another, and the fingers outstretched.

❖ Now bring your hands together very slowly but don't let them touch.

✤ Pull your hands apart and bring them together repeatedly, as if you were shaping something soft and elastic like a balloon between your hands. You should be able to feel the subtle energy field as something like an invisible force field.

✤ If you don't feel anything at first, try making a small circle with one finger around your third eye chakra, in the centre of your forehead. You should feel a tickling sensation as you stimulate the pineal gland and awaken your psychic senses. Then try bringing your hands together again as described above.

Exercise: seeing the first layer of the aura

There are believed to be seven layers of the aura. The more sensitive you become, the more layers you will be able to see. The first layer is the etheric field, which extends two centimetres (one inch) or so around the body. It is the densest level of energy and therefore the first level you are likely to see when you begin your exploration.

Ideally, the lighting should be low for this exercise, and your hand placed on a table or flat surface in front of a plain background, preferably white.

✤ Breathe deeply and steadily. When you feel suitably relaxed, extend one hand with the palm downwards at a comfortable distance, as if you were reading a book or magazine.

✤ Now soften your gaze until you are looking past your hand to the surface of the table, so that your hand appears out of focus. If you are holding your hand in front of you, look to a point in the middle distance.

✤ After a few minutes you should begin to see a fine outline of electric blue light surrounding your fingers. See if you can sustain this soft focus for a few minutes.

Psychometry

Psychometry is the capacity to obtain intuitive impressions of a person by tuning in to an object they have handled. Metallic items such as watches and jewellery are ideal objects to work with as they readily absorb mental and emotional energy and retain the charge over a long period. However, a highly sensitive psychic can 'read' impressions from a flower or a photograph if their client has handled it just before the session. Psychometry is one of the simplest and most easily acquired of all the psychic abilities. If you want to train yourself to do it, or if you want to find out if you already possess the ability, try the following exercise.

Exercise: personal impressions

Ask a friend, colleague or family member to obtain a personal item from someone they know well, so that they can later verify the impressions you receive. The item should be handled only by the owner, so they should wrap it in a cloth or place it in a box or bag before passing it on.

Before you handle the object, relax and quieten your mind. Then take the object in your palm and cover it with the other hand until you feel a warmth or tingling sensation. Close your eyes and keep your mind a blank. Accept whatever images come spontaneously to mind. If a scene presents itself, enter the picture and allow it to lead you deeper into the environment. While you are doing this, describe what you see to the person who brought you the object so that they can keep a record to be checked by its owner.

Psychometry is a talent that intensifies with experience and one that has been called upon by archaeologists searching for artefacts and also by the police, who have obtained vital clues from information gleaned by psychics from the personal possessions of murder victims and missing persons.

10

Kabbalah and Divination

Divination, or fortune-telling, has been practised by Jewish magicians, seers and psychics for centuries, the most celebrated practitioner being Nostradamus – this despite the fact that it is expressly forbidden in Kabbalah. For some, visions come involuntarily, either through an empathic link with the person whose future is revealed or in an off-guard moment when their consciousness transcends time and space. Others develop their latent faculty by using Tarot cards, a crystal ball or runes to stimulate their third eye. But there is another aspect of divination that is rarely explored, and that is its role in gaining personal insight and self-awareness.

The Tarot and the Tree of Life

The origin of the Tarot cards and their connection with the Kabbalah has been a perennial source of speculation, much of it spurious and ill-informed. The truth is that nobody knows for certain when the Tarot pack was created or by whom and for what purpose. The consensus is that it originated in the Middle East during the 15th century and was used for divination, but I suspect that the cards were devised as a Kabbalistic teaching tool – or visual aid, as we would call it today – as the correlation between the Tarot and the Tree of Life is too remarkable to be coincidental. The vivid images would have helped to impress the scheme on the unconscious mind of the student and so facilitated exploration of the symbolic landscape of the inner worlds in pathworking visualisations. The Tarot's use in fortune-telling appears to have developed after the cards were adopted by the Romany peoples and Christian occultists, who found them uncannily accurate for making predictions, an aspect the creators of the cards would not have exploited, as foretelling the future is explicitly forbidden in Kabbalah.

It is significant that there are four suits (most commonly called wands, swords, cups and pentacles) corresponding to each of the Four Worlds (Emanation, Creation, Formation and Action) and that each suit is comprised of ten cards, one for each sefirah, plus a King, Queen, Knight and Page representing the four elements (fire, air, water and earth). These four trumps (picture cards) and the ten number cards are collectively known as the Minor Arcana.

The 22 trumps

The 22 trumps of the Major Arcana are commonly assigned to the 22 paths connecting the sefirot on the Tree of Life, but everybody who has written on the subject appears to have a different system. There is no agreement on which card should be assigned to which path. In my scheme, which is based on sound Kabbalistic principles, the paths symbolise the stages of increasing self-awareness leading to self-realisation.

As such, the cards on the lower triad represent the forces of the physical universe. The first card, the Wheel of Fortune, represents karma, the law of cause and effect, and the second, the Fool, free will and self-determination. Together these complementary impulses find equilibrium in the quality of discernment, symbolised by the World.

On either side of the sphere of Yesod are the Hermit, symbolising humility, curiosity and the search for self-awareness, and the Tower, representing arrogance, false pride and ambition.

The Lovers symbolises the conflict between the intellect and the emotions, while the Hanged Man occupies the vertical path between the ego and the Higher Self, personifying self-doubt and indecision.

In traditional tarot readings, the Devil is interpreted as being a negative sign, but it is my understanding that we have nothing to be afraid of but our own fears and doubts. Therefore in my scheme the Devil personifies self-deception and enslavement. The most common forms of enslavement are addictions, the obsessive accumulation of material possessions and the restless compulsion to prove ourselves, all of which can cost us our health and relationships.

If we can resist this impulse and instead trust in our intuition, we can connect with the Higher Self and channel the life force (the Sun), resulting in increasing self-confidence and a sense of well-being. This awakening invariably leads to the development of an acute sensitivity, or psychic sixth sense (represented by the Moon). In psychological terms, the Moon and the Sun symbolise the qualities of reflection and worldly wisdom, while the Star symbolises the inner light guiding us away from self-centred gratification and desire to unconditional love and compassion.

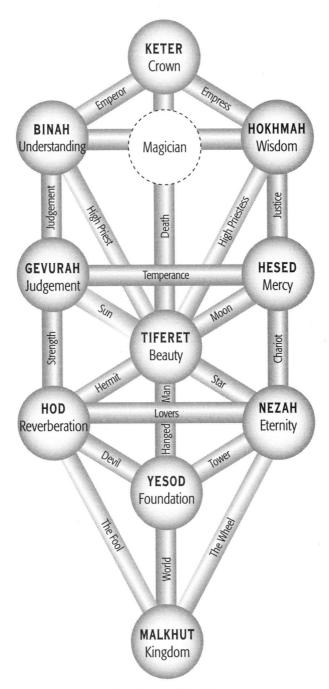

The Tarot and the Tree

Continuing the ascent up the Tree, we come to the card known as Temperance, which is to be found between the spheres of Judgement and Mercy, and so can be interpreted as representing the qualities of restraint and moderation.

I have assigned the High Priest and the Priestess to the paths extending right and left from Tiferet to Binah and Hokhmah, which equate with the acquisition of spiritual knowledge (Priestess) and its practical application (High Priest), which lead to wisdom and understanding.

The Death card is placed on the path leading to Daat, the unmanifest attribute of Higher Knowledge, to indicate the death of the self, which is a prerequisite for union with the divine. Death, the Devil and the Tower need to be seen as self-defeating impulses and not as ill omens randomly dealt to us by fate.

Having overcome our limitations and faced our fears, we become Adam Kadmon (the Magician), the fully realised human being who has command over the Four Worlds within and is therefore the master of his own fate.

Completing the supernal triad are the Emperor and the Empress, symbolising the reconciliation of the male and female principles within each of us.

Beneath them on the outer pillars in order of descent are the cards of Judgement and Justice, the Chariot and Strength. In the individual, Judgement equates with decision-making, evaluation, strength of will and resolve; Justice is expressed as honesty, integrity and sincerity; the Chariot can be interpreted as confidence and self-reliance; while Strength is equated with conviction, commitment and self-discipline.

It is significant that the cards I have assigned to the outer paths reflect the structure of society as an expression of the group soul, with the heads of state (symbolised by the Emperor and the Empress) overseeing the law of the land (Justice and Judgement), which is enforced by the authorities with the consent of society (the Chariot and Strength), resulting in order and stability – as it does in the individual who manages to balance all of these complementary attributes.

A note on the Hebrew alphabet

The 22 letters of the Hebrew *alef-bet* are considered sacred. It is through the utterance of these letters that the cosmos is said to have come into existence, beginning with the primal Yod. The Yod takes the form of a small mark similar to an apostrophe, and all the other letters are extensions of it. For this reason, the sound, shape and pictographic meaning of each letter has a special significance. Heh, for example, is thought to represent the passive feminine principle symbolised by the womb, Yod being the male seed and Vav the phallus. In combination, they spell the secret name of God, known as the Tetragrammaton (meaning 'name of four letters' i.e. YHYH, pronounced Yahweh), and symbolise the union of opposites, which is the central theme of Kabbalah. The study of the esoteric meaning of the alef-bet is beyond the scope of this work, but those who wish to pursue this path can consult the titles recommended in the bibliography.

From Yod emerged the three 'mother' letters (Alef, Mem and Shin), which represent the elements air, water and fire and the three Worlds that they symbolise, the Worlds of Emanation, Creation and Formation. There is no letter designated to our physical dimension.

In addition there are seven 'double' letters (Bet, Gimel, Dalet, Caph, Peh, Resh and Tov), so called because their sound and value can be altered by the addition of a dot called a *daghesh*. In this way Peh, for example, will be pronounced as either 'p' or 'ph'. Resh is the exception; it has no alternative pronunciation.

The seven double letters have traditionally each been assigned to one of the seven major celestial bodies (Moon, Mercury, Venus, Sun, Mars, Jupiter and Saturn). The remaining 12 single letters have each been assigned to one of the signs of the zodiac, although sources disagree as to which planet or sign should be assigned to which letter.

There is confusion too as to which letter should be assigned to which path on the Tree. The diagram on page 106 gives the most common and generally accepted version, but I find it flawed. For a tradition that prides itself on being a logical extension of natural and universal laws, it seems illogical to have Alef (Ox) at the top of the Tree and Resh (Head) at the bottom merely because Alef is assumed to be the first letter. Surely Yod is a more logical choice, for the reasons already given. In Kabbalah the ascent back up the Tree to the source is the prime purpose of life; therefore the alef-bet might make more sense in reverse. This would give us Alef (Ox), Gimel (Camel) and Bet (House) as symbols of the physical dimension, and Resh (Head) in a more logical position, as we know that the ancients considered the Tree in terms of the human body. The diagram on page 107 illustrates my personal interpretation of the letters and their corresponding paths, for comparison.

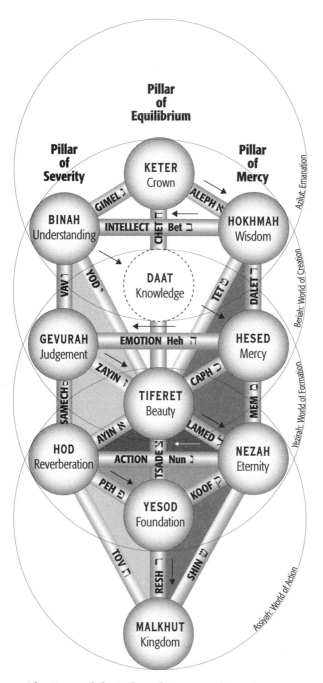

The Tree and the Hebrew letters – traditional version

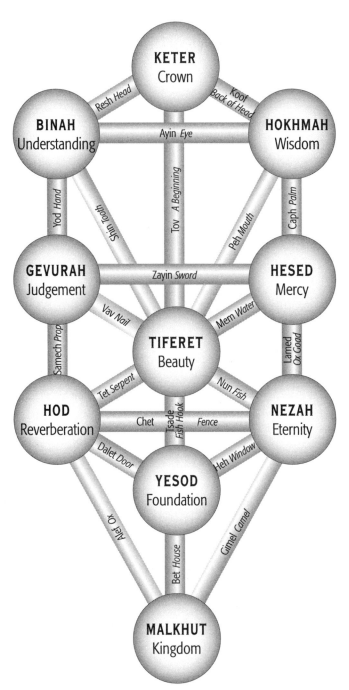

The Tree and the Hebrew letters – my version

Contemplating the Tree in this way is one of the most rewarding and revealing aspects of theoretical Kabbalah and one which I would encourage you to undertake, as you will learn far more from using your own intuition than you will by simply digesting the conventional theory.

Kabbalah cards

If you are serious about Kabbalah, you will need to work with the system on a daily basis. One of the most instructive and enjoyable ways of doing this is to make yourself a set of Kabbalah cards, which you can use for divination and meditation.

There are a number of Kabbalah packs on the market, but they are essentially traditional Tarot cards with a Kabbalistic element tacked on. The Kabbalah cards that you are going to make are unique in that they are an expression of sound kabbalistic principles. They do not predict events as random episodes in our lives, but instead provide a psychological and spiritual profile of the person consulting the cards, using the pictographic meaning of the Hebrew letters. In this way the cards explain why we encounter particular problems, what lessons they are trying to teach us and how we can use them for greater self-awareness and spiritual growth.

The pack can also be used as a visual aid for a journey of self-exploration using the Kabbalistic Tree of Life as a symbolic map of the psyche.

Uses of the cards

Kabbalah has a reputation for being archaic, impenetrable and even deliberately obscure, and so I created the Kabbalah cards as a form of visual aid to help students to become familiar with the system and find a practical application. By using the cards in spreads similar to those used in Tarot readings, anyone who wishes to can discover the underlying themes of their life and the means by which they can overcome difficulties and make the most of their opportunities. There are a number of practical ways in which you can use the cards.

Personal growth and self-awareness

In the beginning it will be particularly helpful to lay out all the cards according to their position on the Tree so that you can appreciate the overall scheme. As you become familiar with the symbols, their meanings and their place in the system, you will acquire a greater understanding of how these divine attributes, characteristics or qualities manifest in yourself. With this greater self-awareness you will be better able to balance your own, apparently conflicting, emotions, impulses and actions.

Meditation

The cards can be used as a visual aid for meditation. You can choose to contemplate one card at a time to access a specific sefirah and then explore that aspect of your personality, or you can use a number of related cards for creative visualisations such as pathworking (see pages 123–9). When used as a meditational gateway the cards serve to access the unconscious, and in doing so will enable you to develop your intuition and seek guidance and insight from your Higher Self.

Divination

Although the Kabbalah cards can be used for divination, they are distinctly different from Tarot cards and other oracle decks in that they do not predict your future as the result of random events, but as the result of the choices you make, given your current circumstances and your personality. In Kabbalah, the exercising of an individual's free will determines their destiny, not fate.

Exercise: Create your own Kabbalah cards

Those of you who have read *Contact Your Guardian Angel* (Quantum/ Foulsham 2004) will recognise these cards as a variation on the angel cards that I describe there. Here, the cards are presented in their purer form and in their original Kabbalistic context, which promises to be even more revealing.

You will need: a sheet of thick A3 card with a gloss finish (to avoid the cards sticking together when you shuffle them) – available from art shops, stationers and printers, some of whom will, for a nominal charge, cut the cards and round the edges for you, making them easier to handle; an ordinary playing card as a template (if your card is not pre-cut); scissors; pencils, felt-tip pens or paints, or magazines from which to cut pictures.

❖ Using the template and the scissors, cut 33 cards from the sheet of card.

❖ Now separate 11 cards from the pack. These will be the major cards, corresponding to the spheres on the Tree, while the remainder will be the minor cards, which are assigned to the paths. The minor cards are used in readings and the major cards in meditation.

❖ To illustrate the divine attributes traditionally symbolised by the spheres, either draw the relevant archetypes or cut appropriate pictures from a magazine (an ox for Alef, a house for Bet, etc.) and paste them onto the 11 major cards. Alternatively, you can simply write the name of the sphere and corresponding archetype, but using images will help you to memorise the cards and will make a stronger impression on the unconscious.

❖ On each of the 22 minor (path) cards draw one of the 22 letters of the Hebrew alphabet, together with its English pronunciation. The significance of each letter can be found on pages 112–15. Your cards are now ready to use.

Key to the minor (path) cards

Each of the 22 minor cards has four levels of meaning, corresponding to the four dimensions in which we have our existence.

❖ The words and phrases relating to the physical world indicate what action needs to be taken in the current circumstances.

❖ The words or phrases relating to the emotional realm reveal the emotional root of a problem or identify the emotional quality needed to overcome a difficulty.

❖ The words or phrases relating to the mental level present the intellectual attributes that are required to resolve the situation successfully.

❖ The words or phrases relating to the spiritual level reveal the purpose and meaning behind a situation.

You will see that the main theme of the card is expressed at every level, so that both obstacles and opportunities provide a learning opportunity for us on a spiritual, mental, emotional and practical level. For example, the main theme of Alef the Ox is 'clearing ground for new projects'. This finds expression at the mental level as 'the cultivation of new ideas', at the emotional level as 'the need to clear blockages or negative conditioning' and in the physical dimension as 'steady labour'.

I have limited myself to a few key words to describe the significance of each card, for the simple reason that beginners can easily become bogged down in detail if they are given a lengthy description that requires them to keep referring back to the book. As a result, they lose the spontaneity that is essential when working with intuition. Once you become familiar with the images, there should be less need for you to refer to the key words.

From then on you will find the images take on a life and significance of their own as you begin to use them as a focus for your own psychic sensitivity and intuition.

ALEF (OX) A time to clear the ground for new projects
Mental attributes: Tenacity, patience, determination and drive, the cultivation of new ideas
Emotional qualities: The need to clear blockages, dispel negative conditioning, overcome self-defeating attitudes and kick old habits
Form of action: Steady labour

BET (HOUSE) The desire for form and structure
Mental attributes: The need to be practical
Emotional qualities: Bringing opposing forces into balance, creating harmony and a sense of security
Form of action: Establishing a firm foundation, order and stability

GIMEL (CAMEL) The means by which you will journey to self-discovery
Mental attributes: Accepting responsibility, a sense of duty, tolerance
Emotional qualities: Devotion and loyalty
Form of action: An act of selfless service

DALET (DOOR) An opportunity providing new insights, knowledge and experience
Mental attributes: Careful consideration and a willingness to face the truth
Emotional qualities: The courage to change
Form of action: Transition

HEH (WINDOW) The need for a balanced perspective
Mental attributes: Vision (i.e. seeing the bigger picture)
Emotional qualities: Objectivity, impartiality
Form of action: Gathering, sifting and assimilating the facts to perceive the truth of a situation

VAV (NAIL) Distillation of energy to a specific point and purpose
Mental attributes: Reasoning, decisiveness
Emotional qualities: Toughness and resilience
Form of action: To join, to bring together and secure, to bring something to a conclusion

ZAYIN (SWORD) Understanding that there are two sides to truth
Mental attributes: Self-confidence, taking a fair and balanced view of a situation, considering the opinion of others
Emotional qualities: Restraint, constancy, fortitude

Form of action: The need to take decisive action to resolve a situation whilst accepting the fact that there may be more than one 'right' way

CHET (FENCE) A boundary to be crossed or to be respected (could be an imagined restriction or a self-imposed limitation)
Mental attributes: Wariness, the instinct for self-preservation, the need for personal space
Emotional qualities: Self-containment, a sense of insecurity and a reluctance to give of oneself for fear of being hurt or disappointed, the need to trust others and life
Form of action: A barrier to progress to be overcome and a time to face imagined fears and doubts

TET (SERPENT) Caution
Mental attributes: Vigilance; be wary of self-defeating tendencies that could undermine your efforts and keep your objective in sight
Emotional qualities: Resourcefulness
Form of action: A time to cast off what no longer has value or use

YOD (HAND) The bestowing of strength or a blessing
Mental attributes: The importance of trust
Emotional qualities: The need for agreement or reconciliation
Form of action: Making a commitment

CAPH (PALM) Prosperity, abundance
Mental attributes: The need to cultivate a sense of self-worth and to be open to a higher influence
Emotional qualities: Importance of being able to give and receive graciously, a sense of well-being and fulfilment
Form of action: Acting in faith, knowing that the means will be provided

LAMED (OX GOAD) Something offering a spur to action
Mental attributes: A willingness to explore a new direction
Emotional qualities: The need to overcome stubbornness or indecision
Form of action: Directing your expertise and knowledge to inspire others or allowing others to learn from their own 'mistakes'

MEM (WATER) A time for overcoming obstacles
Mental attributes: Clear thinking, willingness to compromise, diplomacy
Emotional qualities: An easygoing attitude; the need to accept life as you find it, being flexible and versatile; adapting to circumstances
Form of action: Letting go, making the best of a situation

NUN (FISH) Accepting the will of that which exists outside your influence
Mental attributes: Being open to ideas, the need to be directed to an end
Emotional qualities: Contentment, sincerity (being honest with oneself)
Form of action: Time to go with the flow but not be swept along aimlessly by the current

SAMECH (PROP) A source of emotional or practical support
Mental attributes: Self-discipline, self-sufficiency
Emotional qualities: The need to keep emotions under control
Form of action: The need to act in faith, knowing that unseen forces are assisting from the other side

AYIN (EYE) Developing psychic perception
Mental attributes: Foresight, self-awareness
Emotional qualities: Aspiration for greater insight and understanding, which needs to be balanced by dispassionate analysis
Form of action: Soul searching, active self-analysis

PEH (MOUTH) A time for self-expression and clear communication
Mental attributes: The ability to communicate clearly and concisely, the importance of finding the right words
Emotional qualities: The ability to express feelings without becoming emotional
Form of action: Expressing ideas effectively in order to convince others of the truth of what you believe

TSADE (FISH HOOK) Indecision
Mental attributes: Faith and the willingness to entrust your well-being to the influence of the Higher Self
Emotional qualities: A tendency to let emotions cloud your judgement or to be unduly influenced by others
Form of action: The need to overcome doubts, difficulties and indecision and seize an opportunity

KOOF (BACK OF THE HEAD) The influence of the unconscious
Mental attributes: Imagination, increasing intuition, inspiration and idealism
Emotional qualities: Self-esteem and self-respect, the need to take pride in your achievements
Form of action: The need to act on impulse

RESH (HEAD) Discrimination and discernment
Mental attributes: Reason, logical thinking and common sense
Emotional qualities: Having the courage of your convictions
Form of action: A time to make rational, informed choices and, having made them, remain firm

SHIN (TOOTH) Grinding down resistance
Mental attributes: Self-determination and resolve; a sense of purpose
Emotional qualities: Fortitude, firmness in the face of difficulties or resistance
Form of action: Hard, prolonged work

TOV (MARK) A beginning or a return
Mental attributes: Innovation or acceptance of new ideas
Emotional qualities: Inquisitiveness, a sense of adventure
Form of action: Returning to a source of strength or the inception of something significant

The three-card spread (guidance)

This is the first of two simple spreads described in the following pages, together with sample readings, so that you can work confidently with the deck from day one.

Note: Unlike the Tarot cards, Kabbalah cards have no reverse or negative meaning, and therefore no significance is to be attached to a card that is dealt upside down. In the event that a card does appear upside down, simply place it the right way up and continue the reading.

❖ Frame the question to which you seek an answer. It should be concise and unambiguous. 'Is it right for me to accept Mr Smith's offer of a job?' or 'Will I be happier if I move to Oxford?' are more likely to produce a definitive answer than 'Should I give up work and look for something better?' or 'Is it a good idea for me to move somewhere else?'

❖ Separate the 22 path cards from the pack and shuffle them thoroughly while repeating your question. (If you are reading for someone else, they should shuffle the cards while asking the question in their mind, before handing the cards back to you to lay out in the order indicated. It is better if they do not reveal the question to you until after you have given the reading.)

❖ Take three cards from the top and place them face up in front of you, from left to right.

❖ Select the key words that are relevant to your question and trust your first impressions. Do not be tempted to get too deeply into the significance of the individual symbols. Consider all three cards to see the complete picture, but be aware that there may not always be a definitive answer. There may be positive aspects to both options. Or one card might act to qualify the answer, suggesting, for example, that you will need to overcome your self-doubt if you are to succeed.

Sample reading

During the time I spent developing the cards I gave a reading to a young woman who wanted to know if she should risk leaving her current job, which was part-time and poorly paid, for another, which was full-time and better paid but only temporary and further away. I drew the following cards in reply.

Each of the three cards was strong, affirmative and active. Taken together, they indicated a definite 'yes'. But **Shin (Tooth)** suggested that the new job would require hard work over a long period and would offer a certain degree of difficulty. This could only be overcome by the querent having a sense of purpose and being determined to make it work.

The main theme of **Resh (Head)** is discrimination and discernment, which suggested that the querent would need to weigh up the advantages and disadvantages of changing jobs from a purely practical point of view (including the extra travel). And then, having made her choice, she would need to remain focused on the everyday practicalities and not worry about whether she had done the right thing or waste her mental energy imagining what might have happened had she stayed in her present job. Resh can indicate a personality that imagines it has to create opportunities by sheer willpower, as opposed to the intuitive type who understands that openings appear when the time is right and the person is ready.

Alef (Ox) symbolises the cultivation of new ground, so a move was clearly indicated, possibly a new opportunity in the querent's current field of expertise. It transpired that both jobs were in the National Health Service, but at different hospitals. Again, steady labour was indicated, and certain specific qualities were required if progress was to be made.

Altogether this was a positive reading and a realistic one, which proved of considerable practical help to the woman concerned.

The seven card spread (past, present and future)

In this spread the first two cards indicate influences in your life from the recent past (the last three to six months); the third, fourth and fifth cards relate to your present circumstances; and the last two cards indicate possibilities in the immediate future (the next three to six months).

✢ Separate the path cards from the pack.

✢ Enter a relaxed, meditative state by focusing on your breath and ask for inner guidance in words of your own choosing.

✢ Shuffle the cards thoroughly, then lay the top seven cards face down from left to right as indicated.

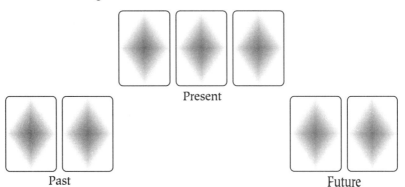

Present

Past   Future

✢ Turn over one card at a time, starting from the left. Meditate on its meaning and record your thoughts on paper before turning over the next card.

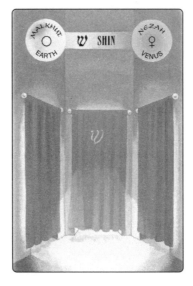

Sample reading

The following cards were drawn at random for a woman who had become estranged from her married daughter and was being unwillingly drawn into an acrimonious dispute with an elderly neighbour, all of which was exacerbating her own sense of loneliness and isolation.

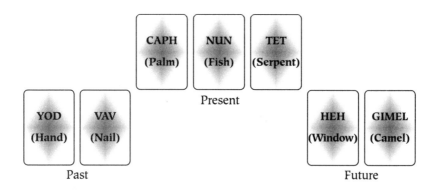

My initial impression was that this was a very positive reading indeed. In the Past position, the first card, **Yod (Hand)**, indicated that the last few months – despite impressions to the contrary – had been a time when the querent had received a blessing or been bestowed with the strength necessary for her to move forward and mature at every level. The 'problems' she described were a challenge, and something that was intended, in my opinion, to force her to reassess her relationship and responsibility to others. I suggested that she had a tendency to 'rescue' and an urge to sort things out so that all would be in harmony around her. Unfortunately, other people might resent that, reacting strongly when their faults were revealed to them or concern was shown. I felt that the solution was for the querent to withdraw into her own space and influence others by example rather than by reasoning. I suggested that some people were not open to hands-on help, but might come around to her point of view if they saw that she was quietly self-contained and centred within herself. Besides, she owed it to herself to renew her energy and re-establish her identity in seclusion. Once other people saw that she had a life that was not dependent on their moods, they might come to their senses and treat her with respect. However, if they saw that she was bothered by how they acted, they might enjoy exercising their power over her.

On a mental level it was a time when she realised the importance of trust – trust in others and in life as an opportunity for experience and growth and not as a struggle or a series of problems put in her way to frustrate her or trip her up. On an emotional level, it was a period of agreement or reconciliation. I had the impression that this may have involved mending fences with family members with whom she had not always seen eye to eye. The card shows a man putting out his palm as if to bless but at the same time keeping a distance from those who aspire to his spiritual understanding and level. My client was this figure. She needed to know that she could love her neighbour while at the same time keeping her distance from him so that she wasn't unduly influenced by his attitude.

That message continued in the second past card, **Vav (Nail)**, whose main theme is the distillation of energy to a specific point and purpose. This indicated that in the past three to six months the querent had attempted to concentrate all her energy on a particular task, such as making herself secure and committing herself to one place after a period of being unsettled.

On a mental level this manifested as the quality of reasoning and decisiveness, and on an emotional level as toughness and resilience. On a practical level, the querent had tried to bring something to a final conclusion, and in so doing secure her immediate future.

The main theme of the first present card, **Caph (Palm)**, is abundance – either material prosperity or an increasing sense of well-being or fulfilment. It suggested that the querent was now moving from a sense of uncertainty to stability. This was a period in which she was cultivating a greater sense of self-worth and so was attracting all that she wanted from life. In so doing, she was becoming aware of a higher influence that had her happiness and best interests at heart.

On an emotional level, she was discovering the importance of being able to give as well as receive graciously. Perhaps in the past she had been too dependent on others or reliant on their support or approval. On a practical level, this card indicated that she now needed to act in faith, knowing that the means would be provided if she followed her intuition.

The theme of the second present card, **Nun (Fish)**, is accepting the will of that which exists outside your influence. On a mental level, this translated as the need to be open to ideas and (as with Vav) to be directed towards a specific end.

Emotionally, we were looking at the qualities of contentment (counting one's blessings) and sincerity (being honest with oneself) so that the querent could make decisions about her future based on facts and practicalities rather than on her wishes. On a practical level, now was the time to go with the flow but not be swept along aimlessly by the current.

This was confirmed by the next card, **Tet (Serpent)**, whose main theme is caution. This signified that the querent needed to be aware of self-defeating tendencies, which could undermine her efforts and her ability to overcome uncertainty. She needed to be vigilant, because whatever she was now aiming for would not be hers until it was firmly in her grasp. It was possible that she used to think she could count on something when she had it in her sights but then saw it slip away at the last minute when she took her eye off it for a moment.

This card indicated that now was a time in which she needed to rely on her own resources and accept the fact that she was not at the mercy of random events or other people's moods, but could create her own reality by visualising what she needed and bringing it into being. If she sought fulfilment, a change of location or work, she needed to visualise her ideal scenario – but without imposing too many details – so that she could attract what was right for her rather than what she wanted, as these could be two very different things.

On a practical level this was a time for her to cast off what was no longer of real value to her – something she may have been reluctant to part with for purely sentimental reasons. It was a time for letting go of the past (whilst still valuing what she had) and moving on. Perhaps she was anxious that she might not be ready for more demanding work with more responsibilities or for moving home, but she was capable of assuming new responsibilities if she could cast off this less confident image of herself.

The main theme of the first future card, **Heh (Window)**, is the need for a balanced perspective. After the uncertainty of the past, the next few months would be the time to accept life as a blank canvas of opportunity for self-expression. The client needed to see the bigger picture and not just her own point of view. Emotionally, she needed to be objective and not see herself as someone to whom things are done, but instead as someone who could let her feelings be known and understood by others. While a mirror is a symbol of how one sees oneself, the window is concerned with how one sees the world and how it sees you. It invites the question, 'What do you project?' The form of action indicated by this card is gathering, sifting and assimilating the facts to perceive the truth of a situation, so if the client felt the need to reflect on the past, she would be wise to do it dispassionately and imagine how she would have advised (not judged) someone in a similar situation

The second future card, **Gimel (Camel)**, refers to the means by which the querent would be journeying to self-discovery. What that was only she could know, but it was something she was doing at present that gave her insight, understanding, and a sense of purpose and identity. The card was confirming that she was on the right path and that she should pursue this direction even though her progress might seem to be slow at times. On a mental level, she would need to exhibit a sense of duty, responsibility and tolerance towards what she perceived to be other people's failings and towards obstacles that she encountered. They were not there to frustrate her but were challenges to test her resolve and opportunities to learn from. Emotionally, she would be required to demonstrate devotion and loyalty, which could involve an act of selfless service such as caring for an elderly relative, giving freely of her time to help others or showing responsibility and commitment, although it might not appear to be recognised or rewarded at the time. It would, however, be noticed and the reward or new responsibilities she sought would be forthcoming.

Altogether this was a very positive reading. I subsequently learned that it was not only accurate but also proved of practical use in resolving the conflicts in the querent's relationships with her estranged daughter and with her elderly neighbour.

Meditating using the major cards

You can safely explore the various aspects of your own psyche by meditating on the archetypes depicted on the 11 major cards (which are described below).

To use these symbols in meditation all you have to do is pick the appropriate card and fix it in your mind. Then close your eyes and take several deep breaths. When you feel suitably relaxed, focus on the image and allow yourself to enter the picture.

Archetypes of the major cards

These archetypes are not to be confused with those described by Carl Jung, the Swiss psychologist, who drew upon mythological figures to embody our abstract qualities or ideals. Instead, these personality types are personifications of the divine attributes envisaged by the Kabbalah. From a psychological viewpoint they can be seen as representing the various complementary aspects of the persona that need to be integrated if we are to achieve wholeness, while on a spiritual level they can be interpreted as symbolic of the stages that we all need to pass through on our ascent to self-realisation.

Malkhut (the Kingdom): The fourth and final stage in the process of creation – our physical world. A strong, healthy man or woman, representing the physical world and confirming that you are at this first level of consciousness

Yesod (the Foundation): A wilful child or an ambitious prince, representing the ego or persona

Hod (Reverberation): A receptive and enthusiastic student, representing the active aspect of our natural intelligence, concerned with communication and learning

Nezah (Eternity): Sensual figures, representing the instincts and also our preoccupation with pleasure and pain

Tiferet (Beauty): A reclining figure, representing the surrender of the ego to the unconditional love of the Higher Self

Gevurah (Judgement): A learned authority figure, representing self-discipline, reason and decisiveness

Hesed (Mercy): A merciful king, representing tolerance, forgiveness and restraint

Daat (Higher Knowledge): The third eye, symbolising inspiration and intuition. This is not strictly an archetype, rather an unmanifest attribute, a chasm we have to cross from worldly awareness to enlightenment

Binah (Understanding): A learned, compassionate and patient teacher, whose uncommon understanding is the result of long study and reflection

Hokhmah (Wisdom): A prophet or mystic, whose glimpse of the greater reality represents wisdom attained through revelation

Keter (The Crown): An archangel, or a blinding white light, representing the divine aspect of human nature

11

Advanced Visualisation Techniques

Having familiarised yourself with the general scheme of the Tree and developed your ability to meditate and to visualise, you can now put the two disciplines together and explore the sefirot in your imagination as symbolic stages in your inner landscape.

Pathworking

Pathworking is a form of guided meditation in which you visualise yourself exploring the paths connecting the sefirot on the Tree of Life in order to experience the distinctive energies of each and there meet and interact with the archetypes who symbolise the divine attributes of the spheres. Such exercises are the cornerstones of Kabbalistic practice. If you are new to Kabbalistic pathworking, it is advisable to start with an exploration of the sefirah on the lower triad, which corresponds to the realm of personal consciousness, before moving up to the three sefirah of the middle triad, the dimension of the unconscious, or Higher Self. Finally, an ascent can be made into the three sefirot of the supernal triad, which represents the collective unconscious. The appearance of the relevant archetype in the scene confirms that you have entered the desired level of consciousness.

If you require an answer to a specific question, or if you want to explore a particular aspect of your personality, you can access the relevant level of consciousness by exploring the corresponding area in this symbolic map of the psyche.

Exercise: pathworking – the inner journey

Before you begin the pathworking, decide which aspect of your personality you wish to work on, then read the description of the corresponding sphere and memorise as much detail as you can. Once you have worked with each of the 11 sefirot in separate meditations, you can start to combine two or more to experience the relationship and interplay between them. For example, you may be finding it difficult to make decisions because your judgement is often confused by your emotions. If so, you will need to explore the qualities of Hod (the intellect) and Nezah (the emotions) in order to reconcile these complementary aspects and address the imbalance. When you have more experience, you may wish to progress through all 11 sefirot sequentially within a single meditation.

❖ Relax, close your eyes and visualise yourself standing outside a vast temple complex. Allow the image of the temple and its surroundings to arise spontaneously. Accept what you see and do not be tempted to analyse the imagery or you may affect the quality of the connection.

❖ Now follow the instructions given for your chosen sefirah, which will lead you into the temple of your choice.

Malkhut (the Kingdom): Contemplate this sefirah if you need to be more pragmatic and grounded.

You enter the temple and find yourself in the entrance hall, standing between two pillars rising from floor to ceiling. The left-hand pillar is of white marble and the right one of black onyx. They represent the pillars of Severity and Mercy, and you now stand between them, acting as the central column of Will and Equilibrium.

Before you is a small altar, on which can be seen symbols of the four elements: a chalice of water, a crystal and an incense burner from which arises the sweet-scented smoke that purifies this sacred place.

In the serenity and stillness you are able to identify the nature of any problems that you may be presented with in your life at this time and what you need to do to resolve them. Think through the practical stages and consider the consequences of various actions to see if they bring about the solution you require. Having done so, you should be able to identify the source of the problem and so avoid such difficulties recurring.

Looking down, you see that the floor is composed of black and white tiles to symbolise the complementary principles in the universe. In the middle, framed in white, is a large diagram of the Tree of Life, depicting the ten sefirot connected by the 22 paths. It is evidently a map of the temple complex, and you are in the lowest sphere of Malkhut. The chequered floor and the two pillars have the effect of grounding and centring you. You have a sense of security and stability, which gives you the confidence to explore this sacred place and discover its secrets.

As the incense clears, you notice three doors at the far wall, each partially obscured by a curtain on which is emblazoned a symbol of the path beyond. To your left the curtain depicts an ox, symbol of physical labour; the central curtain depicts a house, symbol of form, structure and stability; and to your right the curtain shows a camel, symbol of the inner journey and of selfless service.

For the purposes of this exercise, if you wish to continue pathworking up the Tree, you pass through the curtain overhanging the centre door and enter the cloistered corridor leading to the inner chamber of Yesod. Otherwise, leave Malkhut and proceed to your next chosen sefirah or close the exercise and ground yourself.

Yesod (the Foundation): Contemplate this sefirah if you need to be more confident and positive about your self-image.

You enter a chamber furnished predominantly in red. The drapes are a deep, vibrant shade of red and the candles on the altar are also red. You find the colour stimulating and feel more alive than you have for a very long time. The walls of this chamber are lined with full-length mirrors, in which you can see yourself at various significant stages in your life – the person you have presented to the world in infancy, childhood, adolescence and adulthood. All are aspects of yourself and all were creations of your conditioning and circumstance. Each needs to be acknowledged. If, for example, you see a playful child who has been subdued by an adult 'you' who believes it is necessary to be serious, rational and responsible at all times, then you may have to release that child periodically by indulging in an activity that is pure mindless fun – or risk creating an unbalanced psyche.

Hod (Reverberation): Contemplate this sefirah if you need to increase your concentration and be more receptive to new ideas.

You enter the inner chamber of Hod, which is a vast library containing written accounts of humanity's search for knowledge in all its forms. The predominant colour is yellow. The carpet and the walls are a warm shade of yellow, although much of the wall surface is obscured by massive bookcases, which tower from floor to ceiling. Each contains leather-bound volumes and scrolls on every subject that has galvanised the human mind since the written word was created. Here are to be found the classics of philosophy, natural history, science and the arts, which have inspired the great thinkers, social reformers and inventors of the ages to further the inexorable progress of civilisation.

Everything you have always wanted to know is here to be discovered. Do not under-estimate your innate capacity to recall facts and communicate ideas. Everything you have learnt and experienced has left its indelible impression in your mind. You have only to enter this study to recollect it.

Nezah (Eternity): Contemplate this sefirah when you need to get in touch with your sensual nature or if you are acutely self-conscious.

You enter the inner chamber of Nezah, in which the dominant colour is orange. It is opulently furnished with oil paintings, whose subject is the gratification of pleasure in all its forms. The flames of incense burners send shadows dancing on the walls, and the air is heady with a sweet musty fragrance that you find intoxicating. Your senses are heightened by the mildly narcotic quality of the scent, and you feel as if you are drifting in a dream that is so pleasant and relaxing that you do not wish to wake up.

In place of an altar, the centre of the floor is taken up with a large sunken bath, whose steaming waters are too inviting to resist. You discard your robe and enter up to the waist, luxuriating in the heat of the water, which dissolves any tension you may have had in your lower back and legs. You take a pitcher from the side of the bath and empty the water over your shoulders, and as you do so any remaining anxiety is washed away. There are scented oils and soaps on the side of the bath, which you avail yourself of with no sense of guilt, for this has all been made available for your use. While you bathe, the sound of mellifluous music drifts in from an anteroom. It is a bitter-sweet, strangely familiar sound that evokes many memories for you, but it also reawakens a yearning for a country you cannot quite recall but which you intuitively know to be home.

When the music stops, you rise from the bath, dress in a fresh robe and satiate your hunger and thirst at a banquet laid out in your honour. Everything you love to eat and drink is there in abundance for you and for you alone.

Tiferet (Beauty): Contemplate this sefirah when you need guidance.

You enter an enclosed courtyard with verdant lawns, flower beds and a large fountain. The lush green foliage and the soft trickling sound of the water brings a deep sense of peace, and you approach the fountain to drink from its pure sparkling stream. As you gaze into the water you are mesmerised by the sunlight glinting on the surface, and for a moment you close your eyes to avoid the glare. When you look again, you see the reflection of your inner guide. Whatever form it takes, it is an aspect of your own personality, your Higher Self, which you can call upon at any time of the day or night and be assured that it will answer.

Gevurah (Judgement): Contemplate this sefirah when you need to be decisive.

You enter the inner chamber of Gevurah, which is lined with dark mahogany panels, lending it an austere atmosphere, which is slightly softened by indigo drapes. Here you find yourself in the role of a loving parent who must decide on the best course of action in a dispute between two of your children, the dispute being a problem that you need to resolve in 'real life'. Listen as one child argues in favour of a course of action that you are considering and the other puts the opposite view. By externalising the argument in this way, you should be able to determine which course of action will bring the result you require.

Hesed (Mercy): Contemplate this sefirah when you need to practise tolerance, compassion and forgiveness.

You enter the chamber of Hesed, which is lined with purple drapes, and immediately sense the presence of discarnate beings, but you have no fear. They are not concerned with you. They are wraiths lost in a netherworld of shadow. As your eyes become adjusted to the dim glow of the torches that illuminate the room, you begin to discern a group of malnourished children huddled around a maternal figure who is attempting to give them shelter beneath her cloak. But there are too many for her to protect. These are the phantoms of fear, famine, poverty, mistreatment, ignorance, violence, addiction, disease, doubt and despair. As you watch, you sense your heart centre softening and a rush of compassion for those who are haunted by these spirits. Now what can you do to put them to rest?

Daat (Higher Knowledge): Contemplate this sefirah when you are seeking inspiration or an answer to a specific question.

You enter the chamber of Daat, which is hung with soft blue drapes, and are immediately overwhelmed by the rarefied atmosphere generated by those who have worshipped in this place over the centuries. It is a place of serenity and stillness, visited by many pilgrims and seekers after truth. And now it is your turn. Come as a child, eager and willing to receive whatever gift will be imparted to you. In the centre, on the altar, is a chalice of azure water. You gaze into it, and as you do so you lose all sense of self. You forget your worldly identity and concerns. They have no meaning in this place, which exists at the border of this world and the next. Look deep into the water as images form in the darkening depths. What do you see?

Binah (Understanding): Contemplate this sefirah when you are looking for insight into a particular problem, or to understand the significance of a difficult situation.

You enter the chamber of Binah, which is hung with violet drapes. In the centre, suspended from the ceiling, is a huge globe of the world. It almost touches the floor, so when you approach it you are about the same size as South America. The detail is astonishing. Every contour of the land is reproduced so faithfully you could almost believe that you are suspended in space above the earth looking down through the clouds. You focus on your own country. Then, as you watch, you begin to see the roads and the rivers in greater detail, as if you were flying overhead. You can feel the breeze on your face and smell the fragrance of freshly cut grass and flowers. The closer you go, the more detail you can see, until you can distinguish your own town and the people moving below. Consider what is important to their lives and the intensity and immediacy with which they live. Can you detach yourself from this materialistic world view? Can you be in the world but not of it?

You draw closer, until you can look down on yourself sitting in meditation. Now formulate your question. See yourself in the situation you are concerned about as if you were watching yourself in a scene from your life. What advice would you give yourself?

Hokhmah (Wisdom): Contemplate this sefirah when you seek enlightenment or a deep sense of peace.

You enter the chamber of Hokhmah, which is furnished with white drapes embroidered with silver and gold thread. The altar is fashioned from a single piece of ivory, and upon it have been placed one silver and one gold candlestick. A figure stands before the altar in quiet reflection with their back to you. As you approach, they turn to see who has entered and you meet their gaze. It is your Higher Self. In his or her eyes you see the summation of all that you have learnt and experienced over many lifetimes. What do you see?

Now you find yourself looking out from the eyes of your older, wiser self. What do you see in the younger you? Looking back, what was the principle lesson of your present incarnation? How was it to be achieved? Ask what you will of your Higher Self and listen as they answer your questions with infinite patience. They will not judge you, nor will they speak in terms of what you should or should not do. The Higher Self knows that what we consider to be mistakes are merely learning experiences. To avoid repeating them we simply need to acknowledge that we created those challenges and difficulties, and to understand for what purpose. This is the meaning of wisdom.

Keter (the Crown): Contemplate this sefirah when you wish to tune in to the divine aspect of your nature for healing or detachment from negativity generated by other people at work or at home.

You enter the temple of Keter, which is open to the sky. Your journey through the chambers of the lower temple complex is now over, and the next realm awaits. Your eyes are drawn upwards to a pinpoint of light in the distance, far beyond our solar system. As you fix your gaze upon this point, you sense yourself leaving your body and rising as light as a bubble through the air. You ascend through the clouds and on past the planets, into the vast stillness of space. You pass the galaxies and the enormous gas clouds from which new stars are born. You see dying stars, the light from which will not reach the Earth for many millennia. You pass into a realm where there are no celestial bodies and no physical life as we know it. Here there is no sound, no movement and therefore no time. In the distance one pinpoint of light stands out in the emptiness of the void. As you approach, you see that it is not a star but a tunnel of intense white light. You are drawn to it by a sense of belonging, of coming home. As you enter the tunnel you sense the presence of divine discarnate beings, who encircle you as you ascend. These angels, or highly evolved spiritual entities, are radiant with joy at your return. You enter a realm of pure consciousness and experience the inexpressible beauty and perfection of the divine. Linger as long as you wish, be receptive to any form of healing you are offered, accept any gift with gratitude. Ask any question, or request any blessing or intervention you require in your life or another's, and know that it will be given in the form and at the time the angels deem right.

When you are ready, return the way you came.

♣ Ensure that you ground yourself well before resuming your activities.

Exercise: visualisation – the pilgrimage

In order to experience the upper worlds, you need to be able to separate consciousness from the body and project it at will. This is not as difficult or demanding as it might sound, for we all have the capacity to project our awareness beyond the confines of our physical body into other realities. We call it our imagination. Unfortunately, we have been conditioned to consider this facility as unproductive, unreliable and of use only to artists and idle daydreamers. In fact, imagination is a divine characteristic, for without it we cannot complete the cycle of creation to bring our desires into being.

In this exercise you will use Yesod's capacity for image creation and reflection to look inwards into the symbolic landscape of the psyche instead of outwards at the world. At first you may find it difficult to visualise the required images and to sustain them for as long as is necessary, but you will develop this faculty with practice, so persevere. But do not be tempted to perform visualisations on this scale more than once a week. If you do, there is a danger you could succumb to Yesod's capacity for self-deception and find yourself addicted to a fantasy rather than to self-exploration.

* Make yourself comfortable, relax, close your eyes and become aware of the weight of your body sitting in the chair (or lying on the bed, etc.).

* Begin by visualising the room you are in now. Imagine rising and walking around the room. Feel the carpet underneath your feet, sense the air and listen for the sounds around you – the ticking of a clock, the birds outside, distant traffic.

* Now see yourself leaving the room, approaching the front door and entering the street. It is late evening. Take a walk around the neighbourhood, again becoming aware of the sights, sounds and smells. You feel comfortable, insulated from the evening air.

* You cross the main road and the familiar scenery gives way to countryside, but you are not alarmed. You find yourself at the entrance to a forest as the moon rises overhead and the first stars appear in the sky. Make your way to a clearing in the centre of the forest and rest. Sleep beneath the stars, far from your cares in the world you have left behind. When you awake it is midnight and you find yourself with a companion. It is an animal guide that has come to take you out of the forest and on to the next stage of your journey. What kind of animal is it?

* The animal leads you across terrain that is strangely familiar to a town you recognise from your dreams. The inhabitants, too, seem strangely familiar and regard you with interest. How would you characterise the town? What is the appearance of the inhabitants and how would you describe their attitude?

* You leave the town and continue your journey across a lush prairie, through mountains and across a barren desert before arriving at the shore of a great lake. Here you rest and eventually fall into a deep sleep. What do you dream of?

* In the morning you awake to discover that a boat is anchored off shore awaiting your departure. What kind of boat is it and what condition is it in? You come aboard and meet the crew. Who are they? You are introduced to the captain. Describe his character.

❖ You watch the receding shoreline as the boat slips anchor and puts out to sea. Observe the crew as they go about their duties. A storm suddenly blows up, threatening to throw the boat off course. How do the crew react? When the storm abates you continue your voyage, arriving eventually on the coast of an exotic foreign land. You observe a distant city and its inhabitants through the captain's telescope. Take your time to look and gather as much information as you can, as you will not be landing here. When you have made a mental note of all that you can see from this distance, the captain orders the boat to return the way you came.

❖ Once ashore, you find your animal guide waiting to lead you back across the desert, through the mountains, across the prairie and into the town you passed through on the way out. Notice if anything has changed since your outward journey.

❖ Finally, you reach the forest, where you leave your guide. Retrace your steps to your own house, enter the room where you are sitting and become conscious of your weight in the chair.

❖ Stamp your feet to ground yourself and then record your impressions for later analysis.

Each time you practise this visualisation the experience will be different, as the images and impressions will alter according to your state of mind. It is therefore important to note significant changes in the landscape, the town, its inhabitants, the boat and its crew and to compare your notes with those of earlier excursions.

The first time I attempted this exercise I visualised a small rowing boat with a hole in the bottom, which signified that I was not ready at that time to embark on a voyage of self-discovery; indeed, I may even have scuttled my own boat in an attempt to avoid having to face my fears. In subsequent visualisations the boat became bigger and the crew more friendly and capable of handling the storm. The voyage became something that I looked forward to making, all of which revealed a greater self-confidence and a willingness to explore.

The wood represents the vegetable principle, and the animal guide your animal nature, both of which help you to detach yourself from body consciousness at Malkhut. Visualising the night sky raises your awareness to the level of Yesod, with the moon being a universal symbol of the unconscious. The town is the embodiment of Yesod, your psychological state, and its inhabitants are the personification of your sub-personalities, who determine how you react to other people and the challenges of life. You may see them as distinct personalities and become aware that some are hindering your progress by urging you to stay rather than face the unknown, while others may assist you on your adventure. Being able to identify and isolate these characteristics can help you to discover what holds you back from new experiences and whether these cautionary traits are sensible or whether they are irrational fears squatting in your psyche.

The sea symbolises your emotional world, and the boat represents your ability to master your emotions. The crew represents the elements at work at this level and the captain is your inner guide, who will take charge in a crisis if you allow him to take the wheel, so to speak, and determine the direction necessary to lead you to calmer waters.

Finally, the distant shore with its exotic city represents the borderland between the upper reaches of the psyche and the world of spirit.

'Active imagination' exercises of this kind are now a routine psychoanalytical technique, but they are not new. Kabbalists and mystics have been practising variations on such themes for thousands of years. It is known that Carl Jung, the founding father of analytical psychology, was familiar with the teachings of Kabbalah and is believed to have adapted such tried and tested techniques to access the unconscious of his clients.

Working with the inner teacher

If you have ever belonged to a meditation or psychic development group, you will be familiar with the concept of the inner guide, who can be contacted through visualisations and channelling exercises such as the one on pages 133–4. But the notion that we each have a spiritual mentor within is not new nor exclusive to the so-called New Age community. In Kabbalah there is the tradition of the maggid, the inner teacher who appears at crucial moments in the initiate's development to confirm that they are on the right path or to bring insights that are beyond human knowledge. They may appear in the form of an angelic being or as an inner voice. In modern Kabbalah we interpret such phenomena in purely psychological terms, considering the inner guide as a stream of consciousness from the Higher Self – which makes it no less remarkable, but means that we can call on this all-knowing aspect of ourselves at will rather than having to wait upon divine intervention.

While connecting with the inner teacher is useful and informative, it is also important to sound a note of caution for the inexperienced, as there is always the possibility of self-deception. In time and with experience, you will learn to distinguish a genuine communication with the Higher Self from the many other unconscious influences, which can distort genuine aspiration into spiritual superiority and self-righteousness.

Exercise: channelling your inner teacher

This exercise can be performed once a day for a maximum of 11 days. Then it is necessary to take a break for a day before attempting it again. Do not be surprised if it takes several sessions to establish a connection, but be confident that it will come. Your Higher Self is constantly trying to communicate with you and will not fail to take the opportunity if you demonstrate that you are willing to listen.

❖ Read the following affirmations and choose one that is appropriate to your current circumstances or concerns:

✳ I am perfect and complete as I am.

✳ Money flows to me in abundance.

✳ I create and sustain harmonious relationships for the highest good of all concerned.

✳ The universe will provide everything I need – there is no reason to fear.

✳ The universe is a limitless reserve of healing energy that revitalises and sustains me.

❖ Now write the affirmation down at the top of a piece of paper.

❖ Close your eyes and listen in expectation of a response for a minute. Then open your eyes and write down whatever came into your mind. If no thoughts appeared, write 'nothing'. If you received what you considered to be meaningless, write it down nevertheless, as this is part of the clearing process. Do not be tempted to analyse what you receive or you risk blocking the flow.

❖ Now write the affirmation a second time, below the comments you have just made. Then close your eyes again and listen for a response.

❖ Repeat this process 20 times or until you receive an uninterrupted stream of consciousness, which will come to a natural conclusion.

Exercise: visualisation – the inner sanctuary

An alternative technique for establishing contact with your inner teacher is visualisation. To access this level of awareness you need to awaken the relevant archetype, residing at Tiferet, which is also known as the Seat of Solomon because of its association with wisdom. In terms of the Tree of Life, it can be seen as the focal point of the psyche, with access to both the individual and and the collective unconscious.

The imagery in this exercise has been chosen deliberately to focus your awareness on the path between the spheres, so ensuring that you arrive at the appropriate destination and minimising the possibility of self-deception.

❖ Begin with a ritual cleansing and a prayer or invocation in words of your own choosing. Then decide upon a question to which you require an answer or an issue that needs clarification and frame it in words that leave no room for ambiguity.

❖ If you are working in a space dedicated to meditation, light the candles. If not, create a sacred space around you by visualising a sphere of pure white light above the crown of your head and draw it down over you so that you are encased in a pillar of radiant light from head to toe.

❖ Now close your eyes and bring the inner sefirot into balance by seeing each coloured sefirah opening, from the root to the crown.

❖ See yourself at the entrance to a temple. Allow its appearance to form spontaneously. Do not be surprised if you find yourself at a place of worship that has no relation to your own faith or upbringing. This is your inner temple and it has a reality of its own. On either side of the entrance are two pillars, one of white marble and the other of black onyx. Over the door is an inscription in stone, 'Know thyself'.

❖ You enter and find yourself in a courtyard floored with black and white tiles representing the unity of the complementary forces in the universe: energy and matter, active and passive, expansion and contraction. Before you, in the centre of the courtyard, is a tower rising into the night sky, its top obscured by clouds.

❖ You push open the door and find yourself at the foot of a winding staircase. You begin to climb, step by step, assisted by currents of warm evening air swirling in from the open door. As you climb, the currents increase in strength, lifting you higher and higher, so that there is no need for effort or exertion on your part. It is as if you were floating upwards in a dream.

❖ You pass an open window and pause to look down at the landscape below. Then you resume your ascent. As you do so, you notice that the stone walls of the tower are painted a deep blue, like the waters of the ocean. As you float upwards, the colour becomes lighter, so you feel as if you were rising up through the depths of the ocean to the sunlight sparkling on the surface. But when you look up you see that the roof of the tower is obscured from your eyes by a blinding light. It is intense, but it doesn't hurt your eyes. In fact, it draws you towards it, because it is not a light but an energy, and it is radiating from a presence that awaits you behind the door in the room at the top of the tower.

❖ You arrive at the top and pause outside the door, which is framed in the light that is seeping through the gaps in the frame. You feel a sense of expectation, anticipation, excitement and also reverence for the source of this energy.

❖ You lower your eyes as you enter the room, for the radiant light is blinding to look upon. As you adjust to the glare, you are overwhelmed by the sense of being in the proximity of a divine presence. You are on sacred ground. It is a blessing of providence to be here.

❖ After a few moments you feel an irresistible urge to look upon the face of your teacher. And when you do, you see features radiating compassion and unconditional love.

❖ Now is the time to ask your question or request guidance, healing or a solution to a problem. You may be given a direct answer or you may be shown a sign. You may be handed a gift that has symbolic significance or you may leave empty-handed. If the latter is the case, know that what you need will surface in your dreams this night or the next, for you have now made contact with your inner teacher and whenever you seek that connection you are never ignored. Whatever the problem

135

might be, if it is important to you, then it is important to your inner teacher, who will help you to see the situation in its true perspective.

❖ When you are ready, thank your teacher and retrace your steps down the staircase to the inner courtyard and out into the world beyond the temple. Sense the weight of your body in the chair, become aware of your surroundings and open your eyes. Then sit for a moment and assimilate the experience before writing about it.

Exercise: attuning to the angels of the spheres

Although angels are confined to the higher worlds of Beriah and Yezirah, you can attune to them by meditating on the Tree of Life, as each sphere corresponds to a different vibrational frequency associated with a specific angel (see diagram on page 139). By using corresponding colours, appropriate imagery and the angelic names, you can create a sympathetic link to a specific angel, because the interpenetrating nature of the Tree offers a means of transforming the angels' vibrational rate to a lower frequency. Although the angels' energy will be diluted in this way, it is still imperative to perform a grounding exercise before you begin.

❖ Get comfortable, relax and focus on your breath. Visualise yourself standing in a forest clearing. Feel the solidity of the ground beneath your feet and then imagine yourself bending down to scoop up a handful of the rich dark brown soil. Feel the texture of the earth as you work it between your palms and inhale the damp earthy smell.

❖ Now invoke the angel of the Earth by repeating his name, Sandalphon. See him emerging out of the forest mist to stand before you. As he does so, lower your eyes to avoid the brilliance of his radiance. You are humble before his presence, but also energised by it, for he comes to awaken the corresponding aspect of the Earth within you, the sefirah of Malkhut at your feet, which will keep you grounded and pragmatic, and give you a greater sense of stability and security.

❖ In the company of Sandalphon you enter the woods. There you find a swathe of bright red poppies. Stride into the midst of them and pick one. Feel the delicacy of its petals and breathe in the heady scent as you intone the name of the archangel Gabriel, which means 'Strength in God'.

❖ In response to your invocation, a light appears before you, and out of it emerges Gabriel. Again, you avert your gaze from his radiance, but you sense the compassion and vibrant energy that he imparts stimulating you at all levels of your being, physical, emotional, intellectual and spiritual. You are now invigorated, motivated and committed to seeing your ideas and plans through to completion. As the angel of Yesod, Gabriel can reveal much about your perception of the world and your attitude towards people and possessions. You can call upon him at any time when you need to know if you are deceiving yourself in regard to something you think you want or need. You may hear a clear answer in response, or you may be shown a symbol or given a gift, whose significance should be self-evident.

❖ With Gabriel and Sandalphon on either side, you venture deeper into the wood. Here you come upon an ancient stone circle overgrown with moss, lichen and a carpet of yellow flowers. You stand within the circle, attuning to the latent energy generated by those who have worshipped nature on this very spot over the centuries, energy that has charged the stones with power. You speak the name of the Archangel Raphael, which means 'Healing Power of God'. As you repeat the name like a mantra, you see a pulsating sphere of light growing in the centre of the circle.

❖ From this light emerges Raphael, whose presence almost overwhelms you, but you manage to steady yourself and open yourself to his regenerating power. As the angel of the intellect (Hod), Raphael personifies the quality of confidence, self-reliance and a willingness to consider new ideas. If you are faced with a decision that is being complicated by emotional issues (such as leaving your family and friends to pursue a new career), you can call upon Raphael, who is the angel of checks and balances and personifies the quality of considered action.

❖ You remain within the circle in the company of the angels as you continue raising your awareness through the remaining sefirot. Next you see an orange light and speak the name of Haniel, also known as Uriel, (the Light of God), who personifies the energy quality represented by Nezah. In so doing you awaken suppressed memories and emotions, which dissolve any blockages and clear all guilt and regrets as readily as dirt is washed away by the rain. You allow any emotions that need to be cleared to well up and wash over you. You are in the company of angels who have only unconditional love for you. They do not judge. They desire only your well-being and peace of mind. This release is Haniel's gift. You accept it with gratitude. As the angel of the instincts (Nezah), Haniel can help you to get in touch with your sensual nature. Meditating on this aspect can be particularly helpful if you need to resolve guilt issues concerning your sexuality or if you are acutely self-conscious. Haniel can also help you to muster the courage to do what is necessary and give you the confidence to act on impulse, which can be very beneficial if your behaviour is usually dictated by Hod, which encourages you to rationalise and justify your actions.

❖ Next, you see a sphere of green and intone the name of the Archangel Michael, which means 'Like Unto God'. As you do so, you may sense your heart centre softening, which will neutralise anger and resentment while releasing compassion for others. As the Angel of Beauty (Tiferet) Michael personifies the inner guide. If you are upset or grief-stricken, or harbour guilt, regrets or resentment, you can restore your sense of well-being and balance by connecting with the sefirotic quality that Michael represents. Calling upon his energy quality will also help you to see the truth of a situation and the beauty in the world when confusion and violence appear to be in the ascendant.

❖ Now you see the colour indigo and intone the name of the angel Samael, meaning 'Contraction of God', which can be interpreted as restraint and self-discipline. As the Angel of Judgement (Gevurah), Samael personifies the energy quality you need to be decisive. If you are inclined to be habitually impulsive or emotional or are easily discouraged, visualising this colour while intoning the name of the angel Samael will help you to restrain your enthusiasm so that you don't rush into something without due consideration. Consequently you will become more self-assured.

❖ Now you see the colour purple and speak the name of the angel Zadkiel, which translates as 'Righteousness of God' and equates with integrity. As the Angel of Mercy (Hesed), Zadkiel personifies the quality you need to practise tolerance, compassion and forgiveness, or to temper excessive self-criticism.

❖ Next you see a radiant violet sphere and intone the name of the angel Raziel which translates as 'Secret of God'. This angel will help you to express your thoughts and feelings more effectively, awaken your intuition and improve your capacity for deductive reasoning. As the angel of understanding (Binah), he can assist you to realise the significance of a difficult situation, the challenge it offers and the solution.

❖ Now you see a luminous blue sphere and call upon the angel Zaphkiel, whose name means the 'Wisdom of God'. This is the sphere of potential, ideas, inspiration and revelation (Hokhmah). Invoke Zaphkiel when you require a new perspective on a recurring situation

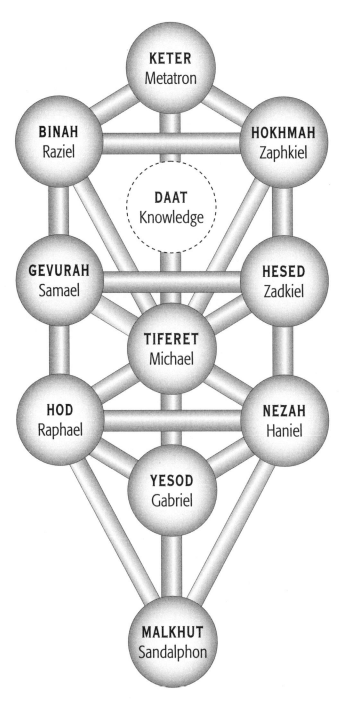

Angels of the sefirot

or you need to identify the major themes of your life and your soul's purpose on earth.

❖ Finally, you see a luminous white sphere and intone the name of the Archangel Metatron, the angel of the divine will, whose name translates as 'Spirit of the Presence'. In biblical mythology Metatron was the first fully realised or enlightened human being, Enoch, whose story suggests that we are all angels in the making. Attuning to this angel of the sefirot dissolves fear; generates a tremendous sense of well-being, clarity and serenity; and is particularly effective in alleviating depression.

❖ You are now surrounded by the angels and encircled with light. Listen to the harmony generated by their collective energy. Feel the vibration of this force resonating within you, regenerating every cell of your being and raising your awareness to a new level of acuity, in which you can perceive the unity of all things.

❖ When you are ready, thank the angels, return to waking consciousness and ground yourself by stamping your feet, rinsing your hands in cold water or going for a walk in the fresh air.

Past life recall

Reincarnation, or Gilgulim (meaning 'wheels'), was a core concept in early Kabbalah but was dismissed as irrational by Western scholars during the Renaissance.

Probing for past-life impressions is comparable to teasing a knot out of a tangled ball of wool. Everything you have ever said, heard and seen is stored in your unconscious and can be retrieved if you are prepared to probe patiently and gently.

Exercise: recalling your childhood

In this exercise, you will be attempting to recall memories from your current lifetime.

❖ Make yourself comfortable, close your eyes and focus on your breath. Begin by choosing a scene from your childhood. It doesn't have to be your earliest memory, but should be one you can recall effortlessly. An incident or snapshot of your life when you were about six years old is ideal.

✤ Now revisit that scene with full sensory recall. How old are you? Where are you? What can you see? What do you touch and what does it feel like? What sounds can you hear? Can you smell anything associated with this episode in your early life? Are you given anything to taste? Is there anybody with you? What is your reaction to them? Take your time. Allow the images to arise spontaneously. Do not be impatient to discover something significant. There may be nothing here that has a bearing on your development or conditioning. Just observe.

✤ Now imagine yourself being tucked into bed for the night. As you relax, you recall an earlier episode, from when you were four of five. Enter the scene with all your senses. Notice what you can see, hear, smell, feel and taste.

✤ Imagine yourself being tucked into bed again and repeat the above process. Go on doing this until you cannot go back any further.

✤ Sit still and, remaining in this state of deep relaxation, look for a recurring theme in your childhood. These seemingly random memories have remained just below the surface of your conscious mind because they serve a purpose. Although they may appear insignificant, they hold the key to a theme that underscores your present incarnation and possibly your previous lives. What is it?

Exercise: visualisation – going home

Having stimulated your earliest memories of this life in the previous exercise, you will now be more receptive to probing for impressions from a previous incarnation. As before, be patient and allow the images to form in response to gentle probing.

There is a chance that at some point during this visualisation you will see someone lying on their death bed and that this person will be you, for it is usual to retain an impression of the last thing you saw in a particular life, and this is often your own body as you gaze down on it at the moment of separation. Such images are often reinforced by the emotional shock that follows the realisation that you have not ceased to exist as you might have been conditioned to believe and that you are no longer the person you thought you were.

✤ Make yourself comfortable, close your eyes and focus on your breath. Visualise a room. It may be from any period in history. Allow the first image that comes to your mind, even if it is a room in your present home. As you explore, you may find that your surroundings change until you have a vivid and stable image from another time and place that will seem strangely familiar.

❖ Examine the furniture. Pay particular attention to any portraits or photographs you see. If there is a mirror, take the opportunity to look into it and observe with detachment what you see.

❖ When you are ready to explore beyond this building, go to the window and see what you can observe from here. What can you determine from the landscape and neighbouring buildings? Are any inhabitants to be seen?

❖ Leave your home and explore the surroundings. Don't forget to look back at your own home as you leave. Follow your instinct as to where you would have gone and who you would have met. Accumulate as many verifiable facts as you can. Look for street names and landmarks that may have survived beyond this period. Are there any notable features in the landscape, such as rivers or mountains, that are likely to have remained unchanged since you lived here? Places of worship tend to remain while the rest of the town is transformed over the centuries, so make a special note of any churches, cathedrals, mosques or synagogues in the area.

❖ When you are ready, return to waking consciousness by counting slowly down from ten to one and becoming aware of your surroundings and the weight of your body in the chair. Ground yourself by stamping your feet to reaffirm your connection with the physical world.

❖ Make detailed notes of all you have observed so that you can verify the facts and determine if what you experienced was a genuine past-life memory.

Real or imagination?

Even if you cannot substantiate the facts of your past life through research, there are several significant factors that indicate that a memory is genuine rather than imagined:

❖ A real memory will appear spontaneously and will often be contrary to your expectations. For example, in one of my own past-life recollections I saw myself in the uniform of a British soldier of the First World War. I was shocked by this vision of an awkward gangly youth, as it was not at all the romantic image of a dashing young officer I would have imagined had I consciously created the image for myself!

❖ A genuine memory will produce a vivid and stable image, which you will not be able to alter at will, and it will allow you to move within its virtual environment from a first-person perspective. If you return to a particular place after exploring elsewhere, you will find that it has remained just as you left it, which is an impossible feat to accomplish using your imagination.

❖ The third and most significant pointer is that the inhabitants of the past will appear as fully developed individual personalities rather than as the two-dimensional characters of our dreams, who often personify one single aspect of our own personality. One of my own experiences highlights this particularly well. During a meditation unrelated to past lives I had a glimpse of a scene in which I entered a synagogue to be greeted by a dozen of my fellow scholars. Through the eyes of my former self I noted that each had a distinct personality that I could not have created in that instant by using my imagination.

Exercise: visualisation – the quest

For this visualisation it is important that you are not provided with any clues as to what you should see or where you are going. You should accept whatever images come spontaneously to mind and follow your intuition until you find yourself at your destination.

❖ Make yourself comfortable, close your eyes and focus on your breath. See yourself setting out on a journey, an adventure into a foreign land.

❖ As you explore this inner landscape, pay particular attention to any unusual features of the landscape, its inhabitants and the weather.

❖ Once you have completed your journey, return to ordinary consciousness, ground yourself and consider the symbolism of your journey. The meaning should be obvious, but if not, you may wish to refer to the key to the Dream Dictionary on pages 83–6. For example, a glowering sky could indicate that you anticipate problems in the near future, barren terrain suggests that you have little hope of success in life, while a steep slope or mountain represents expectation of difficulties ahead. Your means of transport is also highly significant. If you found yourself walking the whole way, this suggests that you see yourself as travelling alone through life, whereas if you are riding on a horse, driving a vehicle or accepting passage on a boat, train or plane, this can indicate that you expect assistance. Remember that the imagery reflects your inner state at this particular moment in time and that the experience will change as your personal circumstances and attitude alter.

Exercise: visualisation – ascent to the celestial city

Before performing this exercise, you should ground yourself by doing the Tuning Up visualisation on pages 40–1.

It should be understood that this is a vision quest, an ascent in the imagination, and not an out-of-body journey to the higher realms, which requires years of study and the blessing of providence.

❖ When you are centred and still, raise your awareness from the physical to the psychological dimension by focusing on your feelings. How would you describe your emotions at this moment? Are you anxious, calm or excited? By focusing on your feelings you are moving your awareness from the Daat (Veil) of the physical tree to the Malkhut (Kingdom) of the psyche. The next stage is to rise to the Yesod (Foundation) of the psychological tree by using your imagination as a platform for an ascent in consciousness. The ability to ascend through the various stages, or spheres, on the Tree is the true meaning of the phrase 'rising in the chariot'.

❖ Feel yourself detaching from your body and floating free. Look down on your body from above. Have no fear that you will become completely separated from it, as you are secured by a silver umbilical cord of elastic etheric energy.

❖ Now rise up and pass through the roof of the building and into the sky. When you have passed through the clouds look down and see the world below. You are now at the Keter of the World of Action, from where you can consider the soil, sea, atmosphere and sun of the physical universe as the four elements of earth, water, air and fire.

❖ In the distance you see a swirling cloud of cosmic matter from which new worlds are born. You are drawn into it and find yourself floating through a miasma of moist air so thick that you feel you are swimming rather than flying.

❖ You emerge in another dimension to stand upon the shore of a beautiful island paradise. This is Yetzirah, the dream world where thoughts take form. You have ascended to the Tiferet of the psychological tree, where the three lower Worlds interconnect (the Keter of Assiyah, the Tiferet of Yetzirah and the Malkhut of Beriah). This is the Garden of Eden of Biblical mythology, the world where all earthly life forms exist in their primal state of perfection. Here, as you wander through the luxuriant foliage, you can sense the vibrant energy emanating from each and every plant and feel the universal force that binds all forms of life together, making each thing in existence dependent on every other. As you watch, the cycle of life unfolds before you. Flowers ripen into seed pods, which drop their seeds. These in turn put down roots and send up shoots, which blossom into magnificent blooms, more vivid in colour than any seen on Earth.

❖ On exploring further inland, you come to the base of a mountain whose snow capped peak is hidden by clouds. You begin the ascent cautiously, one step at a time, securing your foothold and looking ever upwards, never down the way you came.

❖ At last you come to a plateau, on which is a hut and a pen for the owner's goats. It is the home of your guide, who will lead you to the summit. Do not be surprised if the inside of his hut seems larger than the outside would suggest or if the interior takes on an altogether different appearance when you enter. You are now at the level of self-consciousness, so remember the details of your surroundings, as they can be a clue to your inner state at this moment in your life.

❖ You are welcomed and invited to rest before beginning the ascent to the summit. What form does your guide take? What does he or she wear? What do you discuss? What advice does your guide offer you?

❖ You resume your climb, now in the company of your guide, to whom you are secured by a thick rope. You soon pass through the veil of cloud that obscures the summit (Daat). You emerge at the point where the three upper Worlds meet (the Keter of Yetzirah, the Tiferet of Beriah and the Malkut of Azilut), traditionally known as the Kingdom of Heaven in the soul triad. Here the air is thin and pure. You may feel a little light-headed at first, but if you fix your gaze on your guide you can draw strength from him to make the final ascent.

❖ High above you gleams the light of the celestial city, symbol of the sphere that equates with the Keter of the psyche, the Tiferet of the spirit and the Malkhut of the divine World of Emanation. You reach the gates to the city. Your way is barred by the guards, but your guide intercedes and you are allowed to pass.

❖ You enter the city, whose layout mirrors the structure of existence. The outer court is a labyrinth of streets and alleyways teeming with life. The inner court has magnificent gardens, leading to a further courtyard of fountains, at the centre of which is the temple. This corresponds to the divine level. In this way the celestial city itself mirrors the Four Worlds. You pass through the outer courtyard and enter the temple, in which the decorations again symbolise the structure of existence. The plan of the tabernacle, for example, echoes the divine plan, as do the people within, with the high priest, priest, Levite and congregation representing the four levels of divinity, spirit, soul and body.

❖ With caution and humility you approach the inner sanctuary, which corresponds to the Malkhut of Azilut, the lowest point in the divine world. You draw back the curtain and are overwhelmed by the intense light and all-pervading presence of the archangel Michael, who guards the Holy of Holies. You can go no further. To do so is to look upon the divine presence and become one with the absolute, from which there is no return. Ask what you will of Michael, as if you were in the presence of God himself, for Michael means 'Like Unto God'. He is the divine intermediary. Ask for a blessing, healing or guidance and know that it will be granted, for you have made the ascent, and your effort and desire to know your purpose in life will be rewarded. Listen and you will know the true meaning of the secret name of the Almighty, I AM THAT I AM. Ask for insight so that you might understand its significance.

❖ Give thanks in your own words for permission to enter the holy of holies and return the way you came. Then thank your guide and ask that you may be permitted to journey with them again in the near future.

❖ Return to waking consciousness and sit still for a few minutes, allowing yourself to assimilate your impressions and appreciate the full significance of what you have seen and experienced. Then ground yourself by stamping your feet and make notes to ensure you do not forget any significant details.

12

Working with a Group

The spiritual path can be lonely and there will come a time when you may feel the need for the support of like-minded companions. If you can find a maggid, a true teacher, you will benefit enormously from their instruction, insight and experience, but if you live outside a major city you may have to form a group of your own.

The benefits of working with a group

Joining a group or forming one of your own has many advantages:

❖ Having a regular meeting encourages commitment, which can be hard to maintain if you are working alone.

❖ Having even a small group means that you will need a meeting place – whether it is a hired room or private house – which will help those who have no private space in which to practise spiritual disciplines.

❖ Even seemingly safe and simple techniques such as meditation and healing initially require supervision by someone who is qualified to act as a mentor. A mentor is not as difficult to find as you might think. Most towns have one or more active healing or meditation group that is under the auspices of the National Association of Healers. Alternatively, enquire whether such a group meets at your local spiritualist church or a Friends Meeting Hall (Quaker centre). Local newspapers usually carry public notices of such meetings, or your local public library may have details on file.

❖ A group presents a forum for sharing experiences and talking through ideas.

❖ Most importantly, over time the combined energy of the group members will saturate the sacred space in which you work and will create a vehicle for raising consciousness – the chariot that gave Merkabah, the forerunner of Kabbalah, its name.

Establishing a Kabbalah group

Although establishing a Kabbalah group of your own may seem like a huge responsibility, it can also be an enormously satisfying and enjoyable activity. Kabbalah is an expression of love, and it is intended that you take pleasure in contributing to the Great Work. Sharing that experience with like-minded individuals is a real mitzvah, or blessing. If you do it in the right spirit, you will reap rewards you probably cannot imagine at this stage in your spiritual quest.

Do your research

Before you start your group, it can be useful to join a local meditation or healing group to see what elements need to be included and how the energy of a disparate group of individuals is focused for a shared purpose. Trust your intuition to tell you if the group is suitable or not. Look for one that has a clearly defined aim and is not simply an excuse for a social gathering for people with a vague interest in the paranormal.

The group leader

Pay particular attention to the leader. Even those teachers who rely on their guides for inspiration should work to a structured programme. If the leader is disorganised, there is a risk that the energy of the group will be dissipated. The ideal leader is a facilitator, who guides and encourages all the members to share their opinions and experiences. They should not dominate the group. A good leader has their feet firmly on the ground and can demonstrate that they take their responsibility seriously. It is better for a group to be led by an organised and conscientious beginner than by an inspired guru figure who runs the group to gratify their ego and pays no attention to the needs of the members. If you find yourself in a group dominated by a charismatic figure who appears to be fostering a personality cult, leave it immediately.

Even if you consider yourself a novice in spiritual matters, if your intentions are sincere and you have the well-being of the group at heart, you may be an ideal founder and leader. The fact that you are reading this book and considering the possibility of establishing a Kabbalistic group suggests that you have the potential to contribute to the work. In fact, it may be necessary for you to be actively involved in a group to awaken your potential. Every novice needs to become a teacher at some point if the work is to bring light into the darkness and confusion of the world. Besides, you will not be alone in determining the development of the group – you will be watched and guided from above.

Guidelines for the group

Every group needs to find its own identity and define its particular purpose according to the needs of its time and place, but if it is to be a true Kabbalistic group, it will need to adhere to the following guidelines:

❖ Meetings should be convened once a week and begin with a dedication to the divine so as to invite the blessing of God on the group and its activities.

❖ Two candles should be lit to symbolise the group's intention to bring light into darkness, and understanding into this dimension from the worlds above.

❖ The teacher should then lead the group in meditation, raising their awareness from the state of everyday consciousness to that of the Higher Self by invoking the sefirot within, from Malkhut to Keter.

❖ Although some groups may carry out elaborate rituals, it is more likely that the session will resemble a seminar, with the discussion of a topic chosen at the end of the previous meeting and considered during the intervening week. Suitable subjects range from questions such as 'Why does God appear not to intervene in human affairs?' to specific themes such as the nature and purpose of dreams. After the exchange of ideas, each member could formulate a question based on their observations and the issues raised. A meditation could follow, in which the questions are submitted to the Watchers – the great discarnate beings who, through enlightenment, have broken free of the wheel of death and rebirth and now oversee the progress of humanity. They are known in the Buddhist tradition as Bodhisattvas and in the esoteric tradition as the Hidden Masters. Alternatively, you could choose to include a visualisation or a pathworking exercise such as those described in this book.

❖ Avoid the temptation to include an assortment of exercises or topics that have no direct relation to Kabbalah, as this is an unnecessary diversion. One major discussion and a meditation will give a cohesive theme to the meeting and ensure that the group is centred.

❖ The meeting should close with a prayer of thanks and an appeal for the blessing of the divine on members present and absent.

Exercise: the Watchers

In this exercise you will make contact with the Watchers (see above) and have an opportunity to ask for their blessings, healing or guidance.

❖ The group members sit in a circle with their eyes closed and focus on their breath.

❖ To raise their consciousness from the body to the level of spirit in stages, the leader takes them through the first three stages of The Four Elements exercise on pages 36–7, ending with the body and the human attributes.

✤ The leader then states that we all have the capacity to expand consciousness beyond the physical body and then continues as follows:

> *Now that the communal level has been raised, I want you to visualise a point of white light at the heart centre in the middle of your chest. See it expanding and radiating an intense energy, which spreads a warm glow thoughout your upper body, dissolving any tension in your shoulders, before it spreads into your arms, your hands and your finger tips. As it permeates your lower body, it dissolves any tension in your back and releases any repressed emotions in your solar plexus centre. Then it moves down your legs, relaxing the muscles in your joints and soaks into the soles of your feet.*

> *You are now a radiant being of light and every cell is saturated with the regenerating power of the universal life force. It radiates from your toes and from your finger tips and forms an aura of brilliant intensity from the crown of your head to the soles of your feet. You are each a beacon of light, and now your radiance extends to either side so that it merges with the person sitting to your left and to your right. The circle is now a circle of divine light, a ring magnified by our combined personal energy, greater together than the sum of its parts.*

> *Visualise the walls of this room fading as the light of another dimension seeps in, dissolving the barrier between the worlds. And from this dimension are drawn the beings of light, which you can see as angels or the enlightened ones who watch over the world. They are drawn to our circle to aid us in the work that needs to be done. We ask that they draw near to bring the blessing of the divine and to guide us in our search for understanding, knowledge, healing and guidance.*

See them now as great beings of light, one standing behind each member of the group. As they lay their hands gently upon your shoulders, you sense the connection with these guardians of the universe and you become one with every living thing on this planet and every atom in the cosmos, each one an expression of the creator. Surrender to this higher will, to the Higher Self within and to the divine as it manifests itself in the world of matter.

Ask now what you will and know that it will be answered. You may receive your answer as a symbolic image or a colour, or perhaps even as an inner voice. You may not receive a direct answer now, but know that it will come in the following days in a dream or a chance encounter or remark.

✤ A period of silence now follows. Then you continue:

Now thank these great beings and visualise them withdrawing to the world from which they came. See the light around the group recede and the shadows and surroundings emerge once again. Draw the light back into yourself and sense the weight of your body in the chair as you refocus on your breath. Count down from ten to one, then open your eyes and stamp your feet to ground yourself. Sit still for a few moments and consider what you have experienced.

Afterword

A New Perspective

Many of our own personal problems and those of humanity stem from what could be called a divine discontent with the way of the world. We are literally homesick for heaven, feeling incomplete and frustrated with life on the physical plane, where there appears to be no justice or fairness, where loved ones can be taken from us prematurely at the whim of fate, while those who are, in our opinion, less deserving, accumulate wealth and power and are even admired by many for their cunning and resourcefulness. A whole generation has grown up conditioned to believe that their self-worth is measured by personal wealth, power, possessions or celebrity and that unless they acquire all four with as little effort as possible, then they are a failure, as insignificant as ants and without influence of any kind other than as consumers.

Being estranged from the source and unconscious of our own divine nature, we are perpetually looking for love but frequently find that those from whom we seek comfort and reassurance are as fallible and inconsistent as we can be.

Kabbalah teaches that such attitudes can be overturned and that we can find peace of mind, contentment and even hope for humanity if we are prepared to alter our perspective and see the world as a school and not a prison. It is true that for some people life is like a boot camp, but Kabbalah considers a difficult life as a challenge, not a punishment, and therefore potentially more productive. We tend to envy those who appear to have an easy life, but perhaps they have earned it, having endured difficulties in a previous incarnation, or perhaps they have mastered the art of avoiding their problems and may be forced to face them in the future, when they will not have the life skills or experience to cope with a crisis.

Instead of living in fear of death, as most of humanity does, and scrambling to accumulate as much as we can within our allotted time, we might consider the idea that each incarnation is merely a semester in the school of life. But unlike a conventional school, which aims for uniformity and emphasises success or failure, each life provides us with the opportunity to learn different skills, develop our potential and make mistakes without being penalised for them. When we cast off our physical bodies we are liberated from the limitations of the lowest and densest level of existence, the world of matter. 'Death' implies finality, that something has come to an end as opposed to returning to its origin, which is the Kabbalistic view.

We need to accept that it is inevitable that in a world that literally worships power, possessions and personality, those who are able to exploit its inverted values will predominate, giving the false impression that greed and a self-serving creed pay dividends. But we also need to be aware that in every generation there is a proportion of highly evolved souls working quietly to raise humanity to the next level. These are the teachers in the school of life. Sometimes they relax their grip and allow the pupils to let off steam, but they remain attentive at all times. At various stages in history these evolved souls come forward and instigate a new initiative that contributes to the well-being and understanding of the group and may inspire others to think independently, as happened in the early years of Islam, in ancient China and during the Renaissance.

At the risk of overdoing the metaphors, if you are to practise Kabbalah, you need to accept that it is natural for there to be periods in which civilisation seems to be moving backwards; this process is like the ebb and flow of the incoming tide.

It is said that we are less than half way in our evolutionary journey, which in human terms means that most of humanity is at a stage of development somewhere between childhood and adolescence. And so it is no surprise that many of us behave like spoilt children or wilful, belligerent teenagers, throwing our weight about and sulking if we don't get what we want. It is imperative that we grow up and take full responsibility for our actions. We have to make a conscious shift from an egocentric perspective to one of mature, detached observation and cease wringing our hands and shaking our heads in disapproval at the actions of others and instead look at ourselves. We cannot impose our will upon others or persuade them by the force of our argument. People resent being lectured and will resist all efforts to teach them in this manner. The majority learn mainly by example. If you appear self-assured, content, positive and in control of your life, you can exert a positive influence on those around you. You can do your bit to raise the consciousness of humanity so that eventually everyone is able to see the divine in themselves, in their neighbours and in the world around them. In this sense Kabbalah is literally a labour of love.

Recommended Reading and Resources

Reading

Andrews, Ted, *Simplified Magic: A Beginner's Guide to the New Age Qabala* (Llewellyn, 1995)

Ashcroft-Nowicki, Dolores, *The Shining Paths* (Thoth Publications, 1997)

Epstein, Perle, *Kabbalah* (Shambhala, 2001)

Gonzalez-Wippler, Migene, *Keys to the Kingdom* (Llewellyn, 2004)

Halevi, Ze'ev ben Shimon, *Kabbalah: Tradition of Hidden Knowledge* (Thames and Hudson, 1991)

Halevi, Ze'ev ben Shimon, *The Work of the Kabbalist* (Gateway Books, 1993)

Hoffman, Edward, *Opening The Inner Gates: New Paths in Kabbalah and Psychology* (Shambhala, 1996)

Jacobs, Louis, *The Jewish Mystics* (Kyle Cathie, 1990)

Kaplan, Aryeh, *Jewish Mysticism* (Weiser, 1995)

Kaplan, Aryeh, *Sefer Yetzirah* (Weiser, 1997)

Levy, Harold, *Hebrew For All* (Valentine Mitchell, 1970)

Roland, Paul, *Contact Your Guardian Angel* (Quantum/Foulsham, 2004)

Roland, Paul, *How To Meditate* (Hamlyn, 2005)

Roland, Paul, *How Psychic Are You?* (Hamlyn, 2003)

Roland, Paul, *Kabbalah Cards* (Urania/AGM Muller, 2003)

Scholem, Gershom, *Major Trends In Jewish Mysticism* (Random House, 1995)

Resources

Way of Kabbalah courses
(www.kabbalah. society.org)

Useful websites

www.digital-brilliance.com/kab/faq.htm
www.aish.com/spirituality/kabbala101/
www.paulroland.co.uk
www.visit.elysiumgates.com
www.thekabbalah.com
www.machers.com

Index

angels of 136–38, *139*, 140
and chakras *39*, 40
and growth of nations 63
and the Menorah 45, *46*
and pathworking 123–29
and personal growth 63
and the Ten Commandments 47
self-analysis 42–4
self-analysis 42–4(E)
self-awareness 34, 35, 58(E), 70
and divination 101
and Kabbalah cards 109
self-empowerment 87–96
self-realisation 24
spheres *see sefirot*
spiritual traditions, universal 75

tai chi 38
Talmud 13
Tarot cards 11, **101–04**
Ten Commandments, The 47, 65
third eye 93, 97, 98(E)
Tiferet (beauty) 40, 49, 50, 61, 76
and pathworking 126
Toledano tradition 16
Torah see Sefer Torah
Tree of Life 14, *22*, **22–4**
and the body 38–40
drawing 31–2
and Hebrew alphabet 104–05,
106–07, 108
and individual growth 63

meditating on 136–40(E)
and pathworking 123–29
and Tarot cards 101–02, *103*, 104
Tree of Ideas 25(E)
Tree of the Body 51, 57
Tree of the Psyche 51, 57
Tree within, the 57
triads 32
and pathworking 123
see also headings beginning 'Tree'
truth, universal 11

universal truth 11

visualisations 10
advanced techniques 123–46
the inner journey 124–29(E)
the inner sanctuary 134–36(E)
the pilgrimage 129–32(E)
recording 12
vision quests 143–46(E)

Watchers, The 150–52(E)
work
seeing the divine in 69
Worlds *see* Four Worlds

Yesod (foundation) 40, 51, 57, 61
and pathworking 125, 129–30,
131
Yetzirah (dream world) 144–46(E)
yoga 38